*The Political Economy of Global*

# Human Security in the Global Economy

Series editor: Professor Caroline Thomas (University of Southampton)

*Also available*

**The Politics of Human Rights**
A Global Perspective
*Tony Evans*

**African Democracies and African Politics**
*M.A. Mohamed Salih*

**Global Governance, Development and Human Security**
The Challenge of Poverty and Inequality
*Caroline Thomas*

# The Political Economy of Global Communication

## An Introduction

*Peter Wilkin*

Pluto Press

LONDON • STERLING, VIRGINIA

First published 2001 by Pluto Press
345 Archway Road, London N6 5AA
and 22883 Quicksilver Drive, Sterling, VA 20166-2012, USA

www.plutobooks.com

British Library Cataloguing in Publication Data
A catalogue record for this book is available from the British Library.

Library of Congress Cataloging-in-Publication Data
Wilkin, Peter.
  The political economy of global communication : an introduction /
Peter Wilkin.
    p. cm. – (Human security in the global economy)
  ISBN 0-7453-1406-6
  1. Telecommunication–Mergers. 2. Mass media–Mergers. 3.
Consolidation and merger of corporations. 4. Globalization–Economic
aspects. 5. Telecommunication–Political aspects. I. Title. II.
Series.
  HE7631 .W535 2001
  384'.041–dc21

                                                        2001002157


ISBN      0 7453 1406 6 hardback
ISBN      0 7453 1401 5 paperback



10    09    08    07    06    05    04    03    02    01
10     9     8     7     6     5     4     3     2     1




Designed and produced for Pluto Press by
Chase Publishing Services, Fortescue, Sidmouth, EX10 9QG
Typeset from disk by Gawcott Typesetting Services
Printed in the European Union by TJ International, Padstow, England

01      02433

# Contents

# List of Figures and Tables

*To Pa Wilkin*

# Acknowledgements

Thanks to the following: All at Pluto Press for the opportunity to write this, and to my colleagues at Lancaster University (especially Andy Stafford, Gordon Hands, Bob McKinley and Mick Dillon), Caroline Thomas, John Glenn, Lloyd Pettiford, Martin Elvins, Cathal Smyth, John Boyle, Nektarios Koulieris, Louise Saxelby, Jan Selby, and Anelka. At the eleventh hour, thanks also to Katriona Gillespie, and finally, to Laura Shaw and my family.

# Introduction

As an academic discipline, international relations has been primarily concerned with issues of state security in an insecure world. To this end the primary focus of research, particularly in the Anglo-American world, has been upon the nature of inter-state relations. This, in turn, has led to a focus upon the ways in which the historical tensions that have existed between competing states can be controlled through either a balance-of-power mechanism (realism) or overcome through cooperative arrangements (liberalism) (Kegley, 1995, Chapter 1; Baldwin, 1993, Introduction and Chapter 1; Nicholson, 1998). The period of the Cold War and nuclear stand-off saw this account of international relations become institutionalised and frozen in the structure of the international system itself, which threatened potentially to resolve these issues of insecurity once and for all in disastrous fashion. The apparent end of the Cold War has, according to many commentators, seen a shift in the focus of concern of both the discipline of international relations and in the actions of the major institutions and actors in the global political arena. In this book I intend to address many of the assumptions that have underpinned these recent developments in the discipline of international relations in order to draw out their implications for human security and global communication. As I will show, the conventional framework for understanding inter-state security in international relations has invariably privileged the legitimacy and primacy of state institutions at the expense of asking fundamental questions about the causes of *social* conflict and cooperation. As is often acknowledged in the literature, the dominant model of world order in international relations often follows a Hobbesian account of state–society relations in which the very possibility of society rests upon the necessity of establishing the overriding power of state institutions. The logic of this reads as follows: without the state there can be no social order, as our rational and self-interested egoism would mean that we endlessly seek to acquire power to render ourselves secure. As power is a finite factor, our security can only be gained at the expense of everyone else in a vicious zero-sum game. What makes me more secure necessarily makes you less so. The 'timeless essence' of human nature compels us to acknowledge this fact and to build state institutions accordingly.[1] During the Cold War the idea of 'for reason of state'

1

became a theme that helped to shape and legitimise the policies of both superpowers as internal opposition was often suppressed, with varying degrees of violence, by the governing institutions of either the United States or the Soviet Union directly, or through subordinate governments or National Security States (Franck and Weisband, 1971; Chomsky, 1982; Waltz, 1999: $9^2$). As a dominant ideology of international relations (as both academic discipline and nation-state practices), these assumptions helped serve to fuel the very crises of human insecurity that concern this book. The complexities of global social relations are simplified in this orthodox view of global politics at the expense of the issues of social power that are central to social, political and economic relations. My main concern here is with the role of the communications industries in the global political economy and the obstacles and potentials that they present to human security. Thus in order to address this question the book considers a number of themes, introduced below.

Chapter 1 sets out to examine and help define the concept of human security in the context of debates on international relations and the important part that global communication plays in this debate. Chapter 2 examines the meaning of global communication in an era dominated by neoliberal approaches to political economy and raises questions about the power of the communications industries themselves over politics, the economy and culture; the implications for human security of an increasingly privately controlled means of communication, and the impact of New Information Technology (NIT) on politics, economy and culture. Chapter 3 sets out the idea of human security in some detail, both as reflected in the work of the UN *Human Development Reports* and also by way of criticism of that work; from there I examine the relationship between communication needs and human security in an era when the means of communication are both potentially more diverse and pluralised than ever before. At the same time, we are faced with a social reality in which power over the future direction of the means of communication is increasingly placed in the hands of a comparatively small number of private actors and national governments. Human autonomy and a free society, I argue, are central features of human security. They are the bases for our ability to make rational choices about social, political and economic life. To this end education and literacy are crucial to human security as tools of intellectual self-defence and development. This chapter looks at the political economy of education as a facilitator of the communication that is a necessary feature of our ability to take advantage of the resources available to us.

Chapter 4 elaborates upon the important role that communication plays in any democratic political process and considers the contrasting methods of organising the means of communication to facilitate the democratic goals of the participation of an informed and critical citizenry. In particular, I discuss the neoliberal account of the information society and its relationship to human security. Chapter 5 develops these issues further and offers a critique of the neoliberal account of the information society and the problems that it presents for those concerned with human security. What emerges from this chapter and the book as a whole is an account of the way in which *private power* in an era of global communication is increasingly able to dictate the direction of the means of communication with important implications for human security. The contradiction between the prioritising of both the national interest (mercantilism) and of the drive for private profit (neoliberalism) over general human need is a major problem for human security. It remains an issue that is shaping debates in contemporary global politics as ways are sought to control the volatile flow of private capital in a global economy (Elliot and Atkinson, 1998; Krugman, 1999). The concluding chapter will examine these issues in the context of the wider theme of globalisation and world order and what this means for human security and international relations. In particular, what becomes apparent is the way in which revived debates about (global) citizenship and civil society place the means of communication at the heart of their analyses and discussion. In terms of need satisfaction and human security, the question that must be addressed is the extent to which a revived (global) civil society is an adequate arena for attaining this goal.

## CHAPTER 1

# Understanding Human Security

## *Human Security and International Relations*

The idea of human security is both a continuation of established themes as well as being a new development in global politics (Heinbecker, 1999: 1). Its concern with human needs means that it is part of a well-recognised debate in the history of political thought and practice that has centred upon the issue of need satisfaction as being in some way intrinsic to the 'good society'. This idea of the 'good society' is a theme that connects all strands of political economy, whether liberal, socialist or mercantilist (Mosco, 1996; Gilpin, 1987: Chapter 9). The meaning of human security is a strand of contemporary debate about issues of global social justice and is in part connected to the work of the United Nations Development Programme (UNDP), which examines a range of indicators on an annual basis as a means to evaluate the state of global human development, published as the *Human Development Report.* In particular, it lists seven main categories for human security: economic, food, health, environmental, personal, community and political (O'Neill, 1995: 9). The 1994 *Human Development Report* stated that 'human security is a universal concern. There are many threats that are common to all people, rich and poor alike, but their interacting may differ from one part of the world to another' (UNDP, 1994: 22). Beyond that the idea connects with recent debates in international relations that have sought to challenge orthodox accounts of security which have tended to prioritise the centrality and primacy of the nation-state as the necessary foundation for political organisation (Heinbecker, 1999; Bain, 1999; Burchill, 1996: Chapter 1; Baylis and Smith, 1997: Chapter 9; Smith, 1995; Halliday, 1994: Introduction and Chapter 1).[1] What I intend to do in this book is to examine one particular strand of thought with regard to human security: its relationship to ongoing developments in global communication. The issue of global communication raises many important questions for human security and the satisfaction of needs that connect different areas of human existence: the political, the economic and the cultural.

In the remainder of this chapter I want to turn my attention to a number of preliminary matters that will help to frame the ensuing analysis. A brief introduction to the concept of human security is followed by an initial examination of the way in which it is tied to issues of communication and in particular ongoing developments in global communication. These issues raise important methodological points for an understanding of global politics. Although this book is not a theoretical study *per se*, it is worth elaborating on a few of these points if only to clarify for the reader the assumptions that underpin the work. Finally, in this introductory section I tie the question of human security to the wider questions of politics, communication and ideas of progress that lie at the heart of much recent discussion of these issues, that is, to what extent are we moving towards a more cosmopolitan global order, structured in significant part by the means of communication (Moisy, 1997: 78; Habermas, 1999: 1–2)? However, I want to begin by giving a concise overview of the idea of human security and its relationship to concerns with global communication.

## Defining Human Security

The idea of human security reflects in part the work and ideas articulated by the UNDP which, through a series of annual reports, has sought to outline a comprehensive overview of key indicators of human development on a global scale. Utilising the skills of a range of economists, social scientists and other figures, it has sought to outline a vision for the future of humanity which tries to adopt

> ... a broad approach to improving human well-being that would cover all aspects of human life, for all people, in both high-income and developing countries, both now and in the future. It went far beyond narrowly defined economic development to cover the full flourishing of all human choices. It emphasised the need to put people – their needs, their aspirations and their capabilities – at the centre of the development effort. And the need to assert the unacceptability of any biases or discrimination, whether by class, gender, race, nationality, religion, community or generation. [Streeton, 1999: 16–17]

In so doing the UNDP has brought into the public arena the issues that underpin the project of human security. In some respects this repeats themes that have been laid down in the postwar period by such international institutions as UNCTAD and UNESCO. It should be stressed that the meaning of human security does not entail the removal of all threats or risks to human life and activity. Such a goal would require institutions of such sweeping power and reach that the infringement to human liberty would be self-evident (Hayek, 1944: Chapter 9). However, human security does emphasise two particular themes that are central to the idea of a world order based upon some consensus as to the meaning of social justice. First, the satisfaction of human needs should be central to the way in which we seek to organise our political, economic and cultural institutions and practices. Second, an integral aspect of human security is the attainment of human autonomy and the possibility of meaningful participation in the institutions and procedures that shape political, economic and cultural life. The second point is important, as it is quite conceivable that more secure social orders could be established in which material needs are provided for by a political system that is dictatorial, whether benevolent or otherwise. To some extent, the former communist regimes of Eastern Europe were representative of such a political system. If social justice is to be a viable goal and feature of international political institutions, then freedom must be a factor that is central to such debates. For legitimate political, economic and cultural practices to be established that link local, national, regional and global relations,[2] it is crucial that the uncoerced participation of autonomous individuals and groups is a foundation for such a system. Such a process is, of course, both ambitious and complex but the need for the democratisation of the institutions that shape our current world order is already a part of the rhetoric of political life (Held, 1995; Potter, 1997; Habermas, 1999). For autonomy to be attained it is crucial that people have the resources needed in order to make rational choices about their lives that they are subsequently able to act upon. Thus autonomy is about both agency and the participation and control that people can exercise over the institutions, resources and practices that shape their lives. I will consider these questions in more detail in Chapter 2.

Human security, then, is a concern with 'the good society', a familiar theme from political economy and one which recognises that it is not enough for the array of local, national, regional and global institutions (the four levels of world order) that shape our lives to satisfy human needs alone. It is also necessary that we have the capacity to influence these structures, procedures and institutions in a meaningful way. Thus human security concerns itself with the maximisation of human needs satisfaction *and* the type of institutions and procedures that would be appropriate for this. This point is at the heart of a great deal of contemporary political controversy as a range of regional and global institutions in recent decades have expanded their power and reach in ways that would seem to render them increasingly unaccountable to ordinary citizens (Held, 1995). This point is illustrated by ongoing global political concern over such developments as the completion of the last GATT Round, the role of the new World Trade Organization in international political economy, the currently stalled Multilateral Agreement on Investment (MAI), the role of the G7 and NATO in world order (Kobrin, 1998). Equally, the movement towards regional institutional structures has created a number of problems for democracy as accountability and the trust of electorates appears to have been stretched too far; this is evidenced by a number of developments in both the North American Free Trade Agreement (NAFTA) and the European Union (Elliot and Atkinson, 1998: Chapter 5). In the European Union, for example, the Belgian prime minister Jean-Luc Dehaene secured executive powers to raise taxes, cut social security budgets and set wage levels without prior consultation in order to meet the criteria laid down by the Maastricht Treaty for joining the single currency (Bates, 1998). Such a trend is far from unique as was evidenced by the manoeuvres undertaken by the Clinton administration in order to minimise opposition from trade unions and their representatives over the congressional vote on the ratification of the NAFTA treaty (Chomsky, 1994).

## *Security and the Study of International Relations*

It is apparent that in the past 15 years international relations as an academic discipline has undergone a significant shift in terms of the range of theories and ideas given expression. As Michael Mann has commented in a polemical vein, this proliferation of theorising often takes place at the expense of detailed empirical research and in a more worrying way can act only to distance academic study from any potentially wider or more popular audience (Mann, 1996). That said, there is merit in clarifying one's key theoretical premises, if only to give the reader a clearer understanding of the grounds from which the writer is working. Thus, it is not my intention to fall into Mann's trap but merely to highlight a few of the more important debates and issues here before turning to the empirical questions raised by my overriding concern with human security and global communication.

Conventionally, security as a concept in international relations has been concerned with the nation-state and inter-state relations. In a critical commentary, Booth defines the orthodox conception of security in theory and practice as:

> ... traditional security thinking, which has dominated the subject for half a century, has been associated with the intellectual hegemony of realism. This traditional approach has been characterised by three elements: it has emphasised military threats and the need for strong counters; it has been status quo oriented; and it has centred on states. [Booth, 1991: 318]

Working from such a premise, the interpretation of international relations is from its inception circumscribed and directed toward a narrow range of actors and their predetermined interests. In this sense it is the 'national interest' that is primary and the concern with 'national security' that is said to shape the behaviour of all

statespeople in the international system, regardless of their particular ideologies or beliefs (Waltz, 1979; Kennan, 1966; Talbott,
1996). The demands of an anarchic international system compel
socialists, communists and capitalists alike to follow preordained
patterns of behaviour that led one noted scholar in the field to ask
the understandable question, 'Are wars beyond our control – akin
to earthquakes in the natural environment?' (Waltz, 1959: 1).

Given that this is not a text concerned with extended debates on
theories of international relations I do not want to dwell too long
on this particular issue, but it is in order to mention a few salient
points here that help to clarify why human security is pitched
against orthodox conceptions of security on many levels.

*Simplicity and Complexity*

Orthodox accounts of security have had scientific aspirations and
present a simplified picture of global politics for precisely that
reason. As Waltz defines it, being scientific means constructing
theories that have four qualities: isolation (of variables); abstraction
(international politics from all other factors); aggregation, and
idealisation (of models of the international system) (Waltz,
1979: 10). As Waltz says, such an understanding of theory in the
social sciences leads to the following assumptions: 'A theory cannot
fit the facts or correspond with the events it seeks to explain. The
ultimate closeness of fit would be achieved by writing a finely
determined description of the world that interests us ... A theory
can be written only by leaving out most matters that are of practical interest' (Waltz, 1995: 75). For Waltz and others there are only
a discrete range of actors and variables that count in any theory of
international politics if it is to be productively powerful in its theoretical aims. For the orthodox view of security and the primacy of
the nation-state, issues of domestic politics are separated from an
explanation of the behaviour of states in international relations.
The pressures of the anarchic system itself shape the behaviour of
states in the most significant way. A neat, simple, scientific theory
will aim to give a thorough and quantifiable explanation of what
drives the behaviour of states in an anarchic international system,
structured by a balance-of-power mechanism.

However, the aspirations of this particular model of scientific
explanation of international relations are fundamentally flawed for
a variety of reasons that I set out briefly here.

*Ahistoricism*
Such allegedly scientific models of international relations are curi-
ously ahistoric, seeming to pay no significant heed to
developments in human history that fall outside the very narrow

range of variables deemed significant by orthodox international relations theory. As Waltz has commented, 'the texture of international politics remains highly constant, patterns recur, and events repeat themselves endlessly. The relations that prevail internationally seldom shift rapidly in type or in quality' (1979: 66). The idea that an explanation of international relations can exclude matters such as the rise and spread of classes, religion, culture, political ideology, industrialisation and capitalism is a consequence of a method which claims to have located the timeless variables of international politics. The limitations of such behavioural analyses are well recognised in social theory, failing, as they do, to draw out the fact that human practices are meaningful actions, not simply meaningless behaviour. When agents act, they are not solely compelled by external forces to a predetermined end but are acting to a greater or lesser degree in response to their reasons, goals, ideologies, ambitions and all of those intentional characteristics that serve to distinguish human beings from other species. A behavioural analysis that aims for such scientific simplicity can attain this only by leaving out of its explanations *all of the very things that should be of interest to us* if we are trying to understand particular events and general tendencies in human affairs.[3]

*Reductionism*

These scientific models of international relations are reductive in their account of political life. By this I mean that they claim to have located the apparently unchanging essential properties of politics that enable us to focus our analysis of international relations upon these few discrete variables alone. By focusing upon issues of state power (largely military), anarchy (the absence of any world government to impose international law and order), the balance of power (alliance blocs between states) and the separation of international from domestic politics when explaining the behaviour of states in international relations, such accounts present us with a thin view of human history that is limited in its explanatory power for reasons that I will turn to shortly. The state is seen as the largely unchanging and central actor in international relations. As a consequence, the meaning of the state and its historical development and variety is largely (notoriously) under-examined. In addition, our analysis of political life is reduced to a focus upon a few abstract properties that leave out the true complexity of human affairs (Griffiths, 1992). The implications of what an anarchic system will lead to are presented in *a priori* fashion by most realists and liberals alike. Because they ground their analysis in a view of human nature seen as being driven by rational, self-interested individuals pursuing power to make themselves secure, it is hardly surprising that they deduce that international relations will, *out of necessity*, be a violent and dangerous realm. There is, of course, no *a priori* reason as to why the absence of a world government should force us into conflict with each other, but that is not the point. *The point is to offer an explanation that justifies the behaviour of states, not one that explains it.* The latter would focus upon the social relations that underpin political and economic institutions, procedures and structures at the four levels of world order. These raise questions of social power and conflict between classes as well as other social groups, and interestingly are rarely discussed in mainstream international relations.

*Closed and Open Systems*
For such scientific models to claim validity in their focus upon the separation of international politics from domestic affairs, it must be argued that the 'international' is a discrete and distinct realm where unique conditions apply. Thus, it must be argued that the international is a realm that can be abstracted and studied as distinct from other levels of world order. By this I mean that only a few key properties (variables) are seen to be important in explaining why states behave in regular fashion in international politics (Waltz, 1979: Chapter 1). While the idea of closed or idealised systems may make sense in certain limited areas of the natural sciences, it certainly does not easily relate to the nature of social systems (Sayer, 2000: Chapter 1). Adopting Waltz's strategy, we have an example of a form of positivist social science with its aspiration to utilise a unified method for the natural and social sciences that leads towards the production of generalisable (across time and space) statements about the laws that govern social order. The problems with utilising such insights in the social sciences are many but ultimately such an aspiration rests upon the assumption that the objects of study in the natural and social sciences are sufficiently similar as to allow the same methods to be used. As James Rosenau once (in)famously observed:

> As a focus of study, the nation-state is no different from the atom or the single cell organism. Its pattern of behaviour, idiosyncratic traits, and internal structure are as amenable to the process of formulating and testing hypotheses as are the characteristics of the electron or molecule ... in terms of science-as-method, [physics and foreign policy analysis] are essentially the same. [Rosenau, 1971: 32]

There is a welter of problems with such assumptions about the social world that have been rigorously examined by many social theorists and I have no wish to enter into an extended commentary on them here (see Sayer, 1992: Chapter 4). Suffice to say that while we can reasonably talk of questions of structure and system in the social world, these are generally phenomena that have significant qualitative differences from those found in the natural world. A simple example will suffice here to illustrate this. Human beings have both agency and the capacity to learn. As a consequence they have the potential to alter their actions and behaviour in line with moral principles, among other things. They are not condemned to behave in the same way over and over again, and nor do they. Unlike atoms, to use Rosenau's analogy, people have a history that they can understand and learn from. The only way in which the scientific neo-realist model looks plausible is if we are to leave out everything that might be of any explanatory interest to an understanding of the complexity of human history, assuming that nothing of any qualitative significance has ever really changed in international politics. At the most charitable, this is a very thin view of human history. In truth, it is absurd. Social systems are not closed systems but *open systems* within which a number of structures, institutions and actors can exercise a range of causal powers. In any given historical period, and at particular times and places, some institutions, structures and actors will exercise more power than others and it is this that we need to give an account of in order to explain the tendencies that prevail. This is the approach I pursue here in my analysis of global communication and its relationship to human security.

*Determinism*

Finally, the alleged scientific approach presents us with an impoverished view of human agency, arguing that the behaviour of states is largely shaped by the anarchic nature of an international system in which there is no governing authority to maintain law and order. This argument suggests that state behaviour is directed by the pursuit of power and security in an international system where the condition of anarchy has prevailed for over two thousand years. Again, the abstract nature of an explanation that rests upon an idealised model of the international system covering two millennia of human history can only be sustained by assuming that all of the subsequent developments in human affairs covering everything from class, science, religion, philosophy, culture, politics and the economy have not in any fundamental way altered the conduct of states in the international system or even the international system itself. This picture of international relations is such a violent abstraction that it presents us with an image of an international system which is able to mechanically produce and reproduce itself regardless of the qualities of the actors that live within it. Indeed, it suggests that the international system has permanence apart from the actions of those actors, an extreme functionalist view that is surely untenable.[4] Any social system is produced, reproduced and transformed over time and space by the actors that both shape it and are in turn shaped by it. The task of a causal analysis is as follows: to explain the emergence and development of these institutions, procedures and structures; how and why they have come into being, and how and why they have changed and/or persisted over time,[5] something that the alleged scientific model of international relations is fundamentally uninterested in.

*Explanation not Prediction*

What this brief discussion suggests is that understanding world order involves recognising its complexity. Complexity does not mean the absence of explanation. On the contrary, acknowledging the complexity of human affairs simply means that when seeking to explain particular events we need to move from particular events to general concerns with institutional, structural and systemic factors and back to the concrete and historically specific examples of particular actors and concrete events in particular times and places. The task is to explain the interaction between the general properties of evolving historical structures, such as capitalism and the modern inter-state system, and the particularities of distinct events. It also means recognising that international relations is not just about the *behaviour* of states, but about the complex and evolving relationship between states (of which there are different types), capitalism (an economic system that has shaped modern world order) and the meaningful actions of social groups (the actors that have made and been made by these wider political and economic structures). Complexity does *not* mean that *everything counts* in an explanation of the causes of war and peace or the threats to human security. Rather, it means that we need to use our powers of analysis to explain the significant factors and properties that have been at the root of particular events. Thus, the idea of theory in social science is qualitatively different to that pursued in, for example, physics. A deep and meaningful explanation is not an attempt to uncover the invariant laws of society, as Waltz would attempt to persuade us. At best, laws in social systems are tendencies, the principles that tend to underpin institutions in a given historical era. For example, under capitalism, firms *tend* to pursue profit. They might choose otherwise, perhaps to produce and distribute goods and services in accord with human needs. But in so doing they will be breaking the social rules that have been constructed by powerful classes and which underpin capitalist social relations. As a consequence, they will go bankrupt and out of business. None the less, the choice is there. As we have seen, though, a range of pressures at different levels tends to minimise the likelihood of such a choice being made. Such pressures are both material and ideational. In open systems this is complicated by the array of countervailing causal mechanisms that might or might not be in operation at any given time. Thus, a firm might pursue profit but its activities might be tempered by state regulation, the activities of trade unions, and so on. Describing and explaining the nature of these causal mechanisms is the task of theory and empirical inquiry in social science, not predicting events that are necessarily open to a number of potential outcomes, albeit a finite number, as structures do enable *and* constrain.[6]

## Evaluation not Scientism

The idea of scientism is a familiar one in the social sciences and reflects the long-held goal of establishing a unified method that can be used in studying both the natural and social sciences (Bhaskar, 1979). For such a method to be implemented, it would have to be the case that the objects of study in the natural and social sciences were in some significant ways comparable. An extreme example of this idea is presented in the quote from Rosenau mentioned earlier whereby states and atoms are seen as being qualitatively akin as objects of study. If this analysis is correct, then the idea that we can have a science of international relations that is as neat, simple and predictively powerful as those generated in physics is a realistic goal. As many critics have pointed out, such a philosophy fails to recognise the qualitative differences that exist between the objects that compose the natural and social worlds (Taylor, 1985). While it is necessary to talk of the role that structures play in shaping social, political and economic life, structures in the social world are not akin to those that we take to exist in the natural world. The structure of a state, to take Rosenau's analogy, is not akin to that of an atom for a number of important reasons. First, states have a history, which means that they have developed and changed over time in terms of the range of functions that they perform, their meaning for the actors who live within them, and the relationship that they have with other states. Second, social objects such as states are meaningful objects. By this I mean that they are not simply institutions whose roles and functions are predetermined in a timeless and unchanging manner. On the contrary, their meaning is bestowed upon them by people and this meaning can and does change over time. A significant part of any social science is to set out and understand the range of meanings and interpretations that are offered about social and political life. If we take the Gulf War as an example of this point, this does not mean that simply any interpretation of the Gulf War goes, that all explanations are equally tenable. But it does mean that we must recognise that different actors will offer different interpretations of the significance of such events, and that these might change over time. The task, then, is to construct the best explanation that we can in the light of what we take to be the facts-of-the-matter, recognising that we are fallible and that better and more powerful explanations may eventually be offered. The goal of such an approach is evaluative rather than predictive: we consider the evidence at hand and construct and defend the best explanations that we can. Our task is not to predict what will happen in human affairs as such a perspective fails to understand the complexity and open nature of social and political life.

*Levels of Power*

The final issue to be addressed here concerns the question of power itself and how it should be understood in international relations. Again, the orthodox view of power in international relations tends to see power in terms of the relationship between states. On the one hand, power is said to be a zero-sum game in which the increase in the power of one state is necessarily at the expense of all others in a seemingly endless struggle (the relative gains of realism). The second strand of orthodox international relations views power as being potentially a relationship within which all states can gain as they cooperate more closely around issues of security and trade (the absolute gains of Liberalism) (Baldwin, 1993; Kegley, 1995). What both perspectives share in common is a narrow view of power that runs through states and their relations with each other. In many respects power and its acquisition is treated as a self-evident and measurable variable that reflects the rational self-interest of the actors concerned. However, such a view does not take on board either the different forms of social power that can be exercised nor the different levels of power that are a factor of social and political life. By contrast, writers within historical sociology have sought to offer empirical analyses of the different forms of social power that have shaped the modern world order. Michael Mann's (1986) work is exemplary here in that he locates effectively four levels of social power:

- Political power – The authority exercised by the state and political parties over general populations organised into particular geopolitical formations.
- Economic power – The emergence of capitalism as a global system and the social structures, institutions, classes and conflicts that it has generated.
- Ideological power – Rather than simply contrasting political ideologies, we are concerned here with the complex relationship between ideas and existing material conditions. Competing discourses from religions to patriarchy have been instrumental

in shaping the course of modern world order by opening up new understandings of the natural and social world to us as actors. This is not to argue that all forms of knowledge are equally valid, of course, but to point out that they provide us with different ways of making sense of the world. Ideas are crucial because they provide us with different ways of understanding the world, our places within it, and both whom we are as actors and how we should act.

• Military power – The role of military power in the construction of modern world order has been pivotal, from the institutionalisation of taxation through to warfare and publicly funded military research and development.

This complex array of forms of social power forces us to reject both the narrow idea of power as simply being an instrument, and the narrow range of actors (essentially just states) put forward by orthodox international relations theory. An analysis of events in international relations might need to utilise any or all of these changing forms of social power in its explanation. The second point to be made about social power is that the orthodox view presents us with a relatively straightforward view of power as something that is exercised and visible and therefore ultimately perhaps measurable and quantifiable. Military capacity is the obvious example here although there have historically been hugely important qualitative issues about military capacity which clearly complicate even these calculations. As writers such as Lukes have argued, such a view of power fails to recognise that it can exist on various levels, not all of them directly visible or quantifiable. That is, we can recognise power by its effects and its potentials, which include the things that actors do as well as the things that they do not (Lukes, 1974; Sayer, 1992; Fay, 1975). Thus power is a capacity that is both latent and manifest. For example, I have the power to score a hat-trick for my Sunday morning football team whether I choose to exercise it or not.[7] In addition, power is not simply a destructive capacity that people and states possess. On the contrary, power is equally a constructive force that enables us to do such diverse things as acquire knowledge and build better communities. The approach to international relations that I am setting out here would seek to draw upon these insights in order to offer a deep explanation of the causes of such phenomena as human insecurity in world order. In this section, I have clarified some of the theoretical assumptions that underpin my approach to international relations generally and issues of human security in particular. I now want to set out the relationship between human security and communication and the range of issues that relationship raises.

## Global Communication and Human Security

If, as I have suggested earlier, human security is far more than simply the satisfaction of what are often termed 'basic human needs', then it is important to flesh out at this stage both what global human security might mean in practical terms and also what grounds we have for making such an argument. It is also worth emphasising that from our current starting point, even a world where basic human needs were actually met would be a dramatic improvement over the condition in which the majority of the world's population currently find themselves (UNDP, 1999: Overview and Chapter 1). The starkness of this situation is high-lighted only further when the inequalities that structure world order at local, national, regional and global levels are also acknowl-edged. The 1999 *Human Development Report* notes that the widening gap between the world's rich and poor has attained unprecedented levels. This inequality is reflected in a swathe of social indicators that divide states and classes in world order. To illustrate: in 1960 the per capita income ratio between the countries with the richest fifth of the world's population stood at 30:1 with the poorest fifth. This increased to 60:1 in 1990 and 74:1 in 1995. Similarly, this inequality has also been deepening within nations whether they are at the core or the periphery of world order. Britain, Sweden, the US, Thailand, Eastern Europe as a whole, China and India have all seen either significant or dramatic deepening in inequality between rich and poor. In the world's most powerful country, the United States, these developments are stark. In 1977 the top 1 per cent of wealth earners earned as much after tax as the lowest 49 million. In 1999, the top 1 per cent earned as much as the lowest 100 million workers (Shalom, 1999; UNDP, 1999). Taking this to a global level the question of power and inequality becomes simply staggering: the world's richest three people possess more wealth than the combined GNP of the world's 43 least developed states (UNDP, 1999: 258). Interestingly, even the Organization for Economic Cooperation and Development (OECD) issued a report stating that the implications of these tendencies presented a major threat to society, surely the antithesis of the ideas of the 'good society' underpinning any approach to political economy (Thomas, 1996).[8] One major figure in international relations has written that, if anything, the modern world order can best be understood as a worsening of the general human condition, and not only in material terms (Wallerstein, 1995 and 1999).[9] A small minority of the world's population has inordinate power over the resources and institutions that shape the current world order – this is a position that is antithetical to the attainment of *general* human security (Hahnel, 1999). Further, this position is reflected in the structure of the ownership and control of the means of communication and the uses to which they are put in politics, economics and culture. However, in order to make sense of this point we need to look at the idea of human security and its significance for our under-standing of the current world order.

We live in a world abundant in material goods and services and possessing  a vast technological capacity which could be used for ending the blight of poverty that has shaped the modern world order (Jackson, 1994). We could, for example, use these tools to enhance our participation in the institutions and procedures that shape the political, economic and cultural aspects of our lives. What causal factors are preventing such possibilities being realised? Answers to this question are central to current political economy debates and the past three decades have seen the dominance at elite levels of neoliberal approaches (often bracketed under the heading of the 'Washington Consensus') with its emphasis upon the role of free trade and markets and the restructuring of the state. I will set out some of the central neoliberal claims in this book and explain why they are ultimately irreconcilable with the goals of human security.

Is human security concerned with simply realising the satisfac-tion of basic human needs? I would argue that it cannot be. The limitations of concentrating on such a basic definition of human security are two-fold: first, such a view flattens out the concept of needs and encourages us to think in minimal terms rather than the maximisation of need satisfaction; second, such a view fails to address questions of autonomy and the meaningful participation by citizens in the institutions and procedures that shape their daily political, economic and cultural lives. That decisions concerning political economy are often taken at levels beyond the public control of democratically accountable institutions only exacerbates this situation. This, then, is not just a concern with the political systems of developing countries, an easy target for the criticism of Western governments now trying to link aid to democratisation, for example (Vaz, 2000; Albright, 2000).[10] On the contrary, the circumstances in the developed world are perhaps *worse* in political systems where political culture is said to be increasingly driven by private power over public, appearance over substantial debate, money over ideals (Bourdieu, 1998). Political systems, largely driven by money and presentation, act to reduce participation to relatively low levels or else displace political activity to that taking place outside formal political structures (Altschull, 1995). Communication, as both an industry and as an infrastructure shaping the organisation of the four levels of world order, has become a decisive mechanism for either the realisation or the undermining of human security. The practical impact of the increase in the influence of private power over political decision making and the control of economic resources is generally reflected in changing patterns of control and ownership of the means of communication. In effect, it has increasingly moved political and economic decisions out of the democratic and at least nominally accountable public realm and into the hands of private actors and institutions whose interests, as Adam Smith noted, are profit, not public need: 'The interest of the dealers ... in any particular branch of trade or manufactures, is always in some respects different from, and even opposite to, that of the publick. To widen the market and narrow the competition, is always the interest of the dealers' (Lubasz, 1995: 49). Thus, in political-economy terms, the complex structure of power between states, capitalist markets and social groups has shifted to a great extent towards the interests of powerful private capitalist actors and institutions in what is often described as global civil society. Power has shifted out of the public and democratic realm into the realm of private power. This is of great concern for human security in terms of both need satisfaction and of autonomy and participation, as the means of communication are central to the shaping of both.

## Global Communication and World Order

> Very little of what we think we know of the social realities of the world have we found out first hand. Most of the 'pictures in our heads' we have gained from the media ... the media not only give us information; they guide our very experience. (C. Wright Mills, 1995)

> More than armies, more than diplomacy, more than the best intentions of democratic nations, the communications revolution will be the greatest force for the advancement of human freedom the world has ever seen ... the biggest of big brothers is increasingly helpless against communications technology. Information is the oxygen of the modern age. The peoples of the world have increasing access to this knowledge. It seeps through the wall topped with barbed wire. It wafts across the electrified, booby-trapped borders. (President Reagan, Churchill Lecture, London, 1989, in Wilhelm, 1990: 140)

The quotes above illustrate how communication is regarded as being an integral part of the construction and organisation of modern social, political and economic life. While it may be self-evident that ideas of progress and politics itself could not take place without communication, what this book focuses upon are a range of issues that the processes of communication raise for human security. Throughout the course of the twentieth century, alongside the rise of modern mass democratic and authoritarian political systems, there has been an overriding concern with the role that communication plays in processes of democratic control and accountability. A perennial theme in liberal political thought has been the potential threat that democracy itself poses to individual liberty and with the fear that the movement towards mass democratic societies would lead to what Mill referred to as a 'tyranny of the majority'. Hence Walter Lippmann's now oft-quoted concern that politicians in mass democracies should be masters of the 'public mind'.[11] Processes of communication have long been seen to raise important issues of power in modern democracies, as control over and access to the means of communication are key mechanisms in the ability of democratic polities to produce, reproduce and transform themselves on a daily basis. The rise of the modern nation-state in all of its forms is not simply a process of the imposition of authority and military power over a given territory and population. On the contrary, it has crucially been built upon the construction of the *idea* of nationhood, national identity and culture, in which the communications industries have played and continue to play crucial roles. National identity and culture are lived things, ways of life imbued with meaning and significance for their respective populations (Murdock, 1993; Smith, 1991; Anderson, 1983). Thus, a concern with the relationship between politics and communication is a concern with the relationship between the institutions that have shaped the modern world and the ideas that have helped to sustain it. There are a number of different ways of conceptualising this issue. Foucault's discussion of discursive practices and their disciplinary function focuses attention on the way in which ideas bestowed by the human sciences have helped to shape modern societies and their notions of normal/abnormal, good/bad, even true and false (Foucault, 1980). Carey's work on the rise of the PR industry and its relationship to politics in the US has drawn attention to previously unexamined issues of corporate propaganda in democratic societies; likewise, the role of propaganda in the construction of modern polities is perhaps the most familiar way in which the relationship between politics and communication is conceived (Carey, 1997). Finally, Habermas's defence of the enlightenment ideal that we can and do learn from history, that there is and can potentially be an evolution in moral beliefs, can be seen in significant part to rest upon the role that the communications industries play in generating something like a public sphere within which citizens can participate and learn from each other (Habermas, 1979). Developments in the past twenty years in communications technologies have emerged in the context of wider social, political and economic changes that have meant that we have moved to a realm in which it is possible to analyse overlapping public spheres operating at the four distinct but related levels of world order, (that is, local, national, regional and global levels).

I am concerned here with what I term the political economy of communication: issues of ownership and control of the means of communication and what this in turn means for the structure(s) of power that exists between states, capitalist markets and social groups (seen in terms of class, gender, ethnicity, race and nation). Given the centrality of the communications industries themselves and of communication technology in the organisation of complex social relations at a local, national, regional and global level, it is important that we engage critically with the issues that this raises for public life and the wider concern with human security. In practical terms, the past twenty-five years have seen the rise of a form of neoliberal political economy that has presented a coherent description and explanation of changes in the global economy. The rise and expansion of major Western communications companies during this period has reflected the extension of neoliberal policies of liberalisation, deregulation and privatisation of markets and industries. It was also the case that these companies were a coherent political bloc promoting such policies and pushing for the changes to political economy that neoliberalism came to stand for. It is my contention that these developments have been extremely harmful for the prospects of attaining human security not only in terms of the satisfaction of human needs but also in terms of the meaningful participation of citizens in the political, economic and cultural processes that structure daily life. This period has seen a dramatic centralisation of private power over the means of communication, in contradiction with ideas of the public interest. Given that the means of communication are central to the organisation of the modern world order, then the means and ends to which they are put are important points of political struggle and power. What the past two decades have produced is a radical extension of the private control of the means of communication, understood not only in terms of the communication companies concerned with providing news and entertainment but also with the way that communications technology itself has been integral to the transformation of political, economic and cultural organisation and practices (Castells, 1996).

The widespread destruction of traditional labour-intensive industries in the West, coupled with the rise of a service sector[12] in which banking, finance and insurance have grown dramatically, has in part been built around the way in which new information technology (NIT) enables such companies to restructure notions of work-time and practice. As has become something of a commonplace in the literature on globalisation, old ideas of time and space in social relations that helped shape the rise of modern industrial societies have been shredded as distance has been transcended by communications technology. Processes of investment and production have been reshaped to new patterns of work-time as companies are able to operate in ways that were previously impossible (Sayer and Walker, 1992).

The changing structure of the global political economy raises important questions of power in the world order that need to be addressed if we are to understand the impact of and reasons for these developments. Key questions that arise include: who introduces these changes and under what circumstances? Who gains from them and who loses out? How does it affect the structure of power between capitalist markets, states and social groups in the four levels of world order? These are questions requiring detailed empirical analysis and much work has already been undertaken on this issue by a range of writers critical of the impact of neoliberal political economy. My concern is with the question of human security and I want now to introduce the way in which these changes in the communications industries are central to the possible attainment of human security.

### Communication, Human Security and the Public Sphere

Noted American political scientist Robert Dahl (1985) makes the important point that massive inequality is a major threat to meaningful democratic practice, a theme that can be traced back to the work of Aristotle. The reasons for this are quite simple. In a democratic system shaped by stark inequalities of power and resources, Dahl notes that the most powerful actors will, to a large extent, be able to use their influence and power to shape political outcomes to their own ends. This inequality of power is even more important in an era when control of and access to the means of communication have become an ever more crucial aspect of political power (Taylor, 1997; Alleyne, 1995). This thesis has important implications for human security as it illustrates the ways in which private interests are increasingly able to exercise control over ever larger areas of public life, reducing the autonomy and influence of working people. The WTO summit meeting at Seattle in November–December 1999 is a classic example of this, with major corporate actors sponsoring the meeting in order to gain access to the ministers involved in the negotiating processes (Mokhiber and Weissmann, 1999). This in turn has seen a shift in global political economy as states pursue policies that are largely for the benefit of private power rather than reflecting wider issues of human need (Merrien, 1998; Rodrik, 1997: 20).[13] This is illustrated by what

Henwood and Rodrik see as the global assault on welfare systems, the very infrastructures that were established in order to guarantee people's basic needs (Henwood, 1997). This inequality undermines the possibility of human security in two profound ways: first, it reinforces hierarchy and inequality as those actors and institutions that already dominate politics, the economy and culture do so increasingly. Thus it acts to reduce the autonomy and levels of meaningful participation that ordinary citizens are able to carry out in their own political systems. Second, these developments have helped to erode the capacity of states to satisfy the needs of their populations at required levels in major areas such as health, education and housing, exacerbating social tensions that were already prevalent (Thomas, 1996; UNDP, 1999: Chapter 1). Thus when the US President, nominally the most powerful politician in the world, attempted to set out what were quite moderate health care reforms in order to extend health care coverage to those US citizens excluded from health care provision, the interests of powerful private insurance and health companies allied with political representatives in the US Senate and House of Representatives were enough to end this proposed reform. Private corporate power and interests can triumph over even the most basic of general public needs (Henwood, 1993).

At the heart of this issue is the idea of the public sphere, the realm where citizens are supposed to be able to meet and (ideally) agree on the important issues of the day that affect them both as a social body and as individuals. The communications industry has played a crucial part in the rise of the public sphere, as Habermas has noted in a major work, precisely because it has provided the necessary tools and actively constructed the idea of a *public* that is able to discuss, respond to and act upon what are perceived to be the important issues of the day (Habermas, 1989). This in itself generates two important issues of social power: the way in which inequality and hierarchy among citizens affects their ability to take part in these processes, and the role that the communications industries play in the framing of issues and the construction of agendas that shape the public sphere. Human security and autonomy depend upon a critically informed citizenry that is able to take part in discussions and act, where necessary, upon the key issues in political, economic and cultural life. The autonomy of citizens and their meaningful participation depend upon this. When we examine the global flow and production of information and communication, we find an increasing tendency towards narrowness of ownership and control of the mainstream media (Hamelink, 1994a; Herman and McChesney, 1997). This is alarming because it undermines the notion of an *open* public sphere that is crucial to the possibility of free and uncoerced discussion and agreement in political and economic life.

The idea of global citizenship has grown significantly in recent years and is very much tied in with the themes that I am concerned with here regarding global social justice, global civil society and the role that global communication plays in these trends (Habermas, 1999). In part, the idea of global citizenship reflects what writers such as Michael Ignatieff (1995) have described as a growing global consciousness, a moral concern with important issues that connect people around the world. This idea suggests that we have become increasingly aware of our moral interdependence and responsibility to others whom we are separated from by vast distances. As Ignatieff suggests, the global media have played a key part in this trend in terms of constructing a public sphere at not just a local, national or a regional level but increasingly at a global one. This sense of totality, the historical connectedness of events and processes coupled with an awareness of the suffering of others is seen by many as being an historically unique development in human affairs and perhaps a qualitative change in the way in which we have thought and will continue to think about politics and society. It also has congruence with Habermas's ideas regarding the evolution of moral beliefs that we can learn from history about what is and is not an acceptable and/or necessary activity on the part of governments and citizens alike. However, the idea of global citizenship raises major issues for established ideas about citizenship; it clearly transcends conventional notions about the relationship between the nation-state and its citizens as being the *limit* of our political obligations and responsibilities. As Linklater has commented, a small but increasing proportion of the world's population sees its responsibilities in international terms (Linklater, 1998). The idea that states have the right to absolute sovereignty over how they treat their populations has taken a significant dent in the past century as it has been used as an excuse for brutal and genocidal behaviour towards sections of their populations.[14] If human security is a concern with the general and particular needs of people at the four levels of world order, then these issues of global social justice, citizenship and civil society are important factors in this development. However, in practical terms these issues all raise questions about the structure(s) of power in the relationships between states, social groups and capitalist markets. In Chapter 2 , I turn to the ongoing developments in global communication so that we can ultimately reflect upon their importance for issues of human security.

## CHAPTER 2

# Towards a Global Communications Industry

The idea of global communication has become something of a truism in analyses of globalisation but remains a far from straight-forward concept.[1] The reality of the development of the communications industry over the past two decades is more complex than such a general term allows for, as even a cursory examination of the prevailing tendencies in media markets reveals. This does not invalidate the concept of global communication, however, as there is little reason to doubt that the global reach of the major communications corporations is unprecedented and represents a qualitative shift in the organisation of global communication.[2] News Corporation is a classic example of a communications corporation that has pursued a strategy leading to the integration of a global network of interests in many of the world's established and emerging markets. Thus, News Corporation is well positioned to gain from economic and political liberalisation in India and China.[3] In order to make sense of this theme, though, and to consider its importance to human security, we need first to clarify a range of issues. Thus, in this chapter I examine the idea of global communication and the communications industry in an attempt to explain why recent developments in technology and patterns of ownership and control have been so significant; I also examine the political-economic reasons underpinning these trans-formations in the industry before turning to the issues that they raise for human security and its concern with human autonomy. I want to begin by looking at the idea of the communications industry and global communication itself.

## Global Communication? – A Historical Overview

> 'The question is how do we best determine and meet the communication needs of a society?' (Stephen McDowell, in Comor, 1994: 110)

In order to make sense of recent developments in the communica-tions industry it is important that we have some idea of the way in which they have developed over the past 150 years. Clearly there is some difficulty in defining the communications industries as distinct agents, as these modern corporate giants are often integrated both vertically and horizontally with a range of other corporate interests that cut across a variety of industries, from arms production to forms of manufacturing and communications services. As Robert McChesney has recently noted, the world's communications markets are dominated by a handful of companies, a global oligarchy. In an important recent work on this topic Herman and McChesney (1997) classify the global media in two tiers:

- First-tier media firms: Global communications corporations – Time-Warner, Disney, Bertelsmann, Viacom, News Corporation (all of which are the most fully integrated global media corporations); WorldCom (which now incorporates TCI), Polygram (Philips), Seagram (Universal), Sony and General Electric.

- Second-tier media firms: Regional communications corporations – There are around forty regional media largely dominated by the US and Europe, though Latin America boasts four regional corporations and more are expected to emerge in other parts of the Third World, particularly Asia.

When I use the term 'communications industries' I include those institutions that provide not only news and entertainment for citizens and consumers alike but also those companies that provide the hardware and software new information technology (NIT) that has been crucial to the reorganisation of the global economy. Essentially NIT can be seen as incorporating telecommunications and computing. Thus global communications corporations can be usefully divided into two groups: global entertainment communications corporations, and global telecommunications corporations.

In this respect we can already see why the communications industries are so important to global capitalism. They provide the infrastructural goods and services needed by global corporations generally to organise their activities over huge geographical distances and to coordinate production in accord with different time zones. As Comor has argued, as a proportion of the global economy those corporations that fall under this sector were producing US$1.185 trillion, 9 per cent of the world's recorded economic output; this is a figure which is continuing to rise (Comor, 1994: 2). However, the view that we have seen a transformation of the nationally based communications industries into global communications corporations needs to be more nuanced. Although developments of the past two decades, which I will turn to in more detail shortly, have created unprecedented opportunities for the communications industries to expand their global reach, it has always been the case that the larger communications corporations

have sought to project themselves and their products internationally (Boyd-Barrett and Tantanen, 1998).[4] What is different now,
qualitatively so, is the sheer scale and planning that the giant corporations are able to project, transcending national markets to target
consumers globally. Previous barriers of time and space which
served as a constraint upon the activities and reach of companies
have been shredded as a consequence of the technological breakthroughs that NIT has brought to global capitalism in general
(Dicken and Lloyd, 1990; Dicken, 1992 and 1998 editions; Meiskins,
1998; Comor, 1994; McChesney, 1999; Sayer and Walker, 1992; Nye
and Owens, 1992; Mosco and Wasko, 1988; Poster, 1995; Locksley,
1986). I will examine this point in more detail later in this chapter.

It is the general intensification of the commodification of cultural
goods and services that has been crucial in fuelling the expansion of
the communications industries as a sector of the global economy in
terms of both employment and wealth created. For example, in the
United States alone more than three-quarters of the workforce are
now employed in jobs directly involving the production, processing
or distribution of information (Comor, 1994: 2). In 1991, the global
Telecom market was worth approximately US $150 billion and was
expected to grow to US $600 billion by the year 2000 (Hamelink,
1994a and b: 59; Mowlana, 1996: 56). What these current tendencies
in communications markets reveal, however, is a tension between
public and private interests over the control and use of the means of
communication. This manifests itself in the struggle among political
and economic elites over the regulation of the telecommunications
market (WTO Paper, 1997; Mulgan, 1991) (see Table 2.1).

**Table 2.1  Top ten global telecommunications corporations**

| Rank | Company | Fortune Global 500 Revenues Rank 1999 | Revenues US$ Millions |
|------|---------|------------------------|-----------|
| 1 | Nippon Telegraph and Telephone (Japan) | 13 | 93,591.7 |
| 2 | AT & T (USA) | 28 | 62,391 |
| 3 | SBC Communications (USA) | 42 | 49,489 |
| 4 | Deutsche Telekom (Germany) | 77 | 37,835 |
| 5 | WorldCom (USA) | 79 | 37,120 |
| 6 | Verizon Communications (USA) | 97 | 33,174 |
| 7 | BT (UK) | 110 | 30,546 |
| 8 | Olivetti (Italy) | 112 | 30,088 |
| 9 | France Telecom (France) | 118 | 29,049 |
| 10 | GTE (USA) | 152 | 25,336 |

*Source: Fortune Global 500, 1999.*
<http://www.fortune.com/fortune/global500/indsnap/0,5980,IN|157,00.html>

To make sense of this we need to retreat somewhat and briefly consider the historical evolution of communications markets and technology.

## States and Mass Communications

The tension between public and private ownership and control of the means of communication has been a consistent factor in the rise of modern nation-states. States have historically tended to act in various international forums to regulate the flow of communication, whether, it be through the International Telecommunications Union (ITU) or the more decentralised structures of the International Postal Union (IPU) (Murphy, 1994; Hamelink, 1994a). The principle underpinning the legitimacy of state regulation of the means of communication has always been based upon the fact that there have been technologically imposed structural limits on the means of communication. Radio and television spectra for example, allowed for a limited number of stations and these needed to be regulated and coordinated in the public interest to prevent abuses of power. This, in turn, has meant states have had to intervene on behalf of the public interest to ensure equality of access and opportunity. States have always found a variety of means to regulate and control the flow of information. On a more benign level they have used such methods as the issuing of licences to transmit or broadcast, and to the use of taxation and subsidies. More coercively states have used mechanisms such as direct censorship, control and licensing (Curran and Seaton, 1997; Keane, 1991). The assumption underpinning state regulation at both national and international levels was that the technology that lies at the heart of the means of communication represented a natural monopoly. As Hamelink has suggested, for 120 years or so there was something like a dominant regulatory framework that oversaw the communications industries:

> The standard of availability obviously demands international co-ordination. It requires that telecommunications networks are technically compatible and that common rules are adopted about access to and use of these networks ... From the mid 19th Century to the 1970s this co-ordination was governed by a stable and robust multilateral accord. The world community had adopted common standards on the technical compatibility of networks and the price setting for access to and use of these networks. This public service type of agreement was based upon the principles of natural monopoly and cross-subsidisation. Monopolies of equipment and services were seen to provide efficient and equitable public service. [Hamelink, 1994a: 68]

The emergence of modern nation-states in part hinged upon the ability of state institutions to use the means of communications to promote ideas of national culture and a common history that could unite a given population within a clearly defined territorial border. As Benedict Anderson, among others, has argued, the *idea* of the nation is crucial to the legitimacy and cohesion of the modern nation-state and it is the realm of communication that has served to disseminate and spread such ideas (Anderson, 1992; Mowlana, 1996: 90–102; Bendix, 1969). This has been implemented through a variety of mechanisms such as education or commonly shared cultural forms such as radio and television (Smith, 1991; Williams, 1984: Part 2; Thompson, 1990). The BBC is a classic example of an institution that has sought to project both political and cultural principles. To this end its former Director-General Charles Curran noted:

> the underlying assumption of the BBC is that of liberal democracy ... Broadcasters have a responsibility, therefore, to provide a rationally based and balanced service of news which will enable adult people to make basic judgements about public policy ... in their capacity as voting citizens of a democracy. [Ferguson, 1989: 84]

States have played the role of regulating the communications industries precisely because it is the state theoretically (however flawed and inconsistent this might be in practice) that serves to limit the dominance of private power over society, what we can usefully describe as the 'tyranny of the minority'. The extent to which states have achieved this goal is a reflection of the pressure bought to bear upon governing institutions by a wide array of social forces acting to protect themselves from private power (Polanyi, 1944).

The 'tyranny of the minority' can be seen as being both an inter- and intra-class conflict. The ongoing Microsoft dispute in the US courts is a good example of intra-class conflict, as the dispute involves a number of powerful actors and institutions in the US business and political worlds over questions of market share and acceptable profit levels. Thus there has always been a struggle both between and among conflicting social groups over the control of the means of communication and historically, with the exception of the United States, the state has tended to play a prominent role in its regulation (McChesney, 1993; Herman and Chomksy, 1988; Hutchison, 1999: 1–124; Collins and Murroni, 1996: 1–35; Lichtenberg, 1990). In economic terms the advantage of state regulation has in part been that it has promoted a standardisation of such things as copyright and codes of practice as well as technology, all of which have served to facilitate easier communication and also to lower costs for the corporations involved (Murphy, 1994).

However, this framework, based upon the idea of communications networks as a natural monopoly that had to be publicly owned and accountable to some notion of the public interest, has undergone a dramatic transformation in the past twenty five years. By the mid-1970s, this framework was beginning to unravel in response to three major changes in global political economy of which the communications industries are one crucial part. These changes reflect a wider and concerted effort on the part of big business to push back many of the gains made by workers over the past hundred years, a form of global class war (Chomsky, 1998). This is as true of the communications industries in particular as it is of capitalism in general. It is to these issues and to this context that we must now turn.

### The Political Economy of Global Communication – Understanding the Transformation of Media Markets

There is no consensus as to the meaning of political economy in general and this dissent reflects the intellectual divisions that have persisted between liberals, Marxists, socialists, Keynesians, mercantilists, and so on (Gilpin, 1987; Mosco, 1996). For the purpose of this book I am taking political economy to be a concern with the structure(s) of power that exists between global social forces, global capitalism and geopolitical institutions, as illustrated in Figure 2.1.

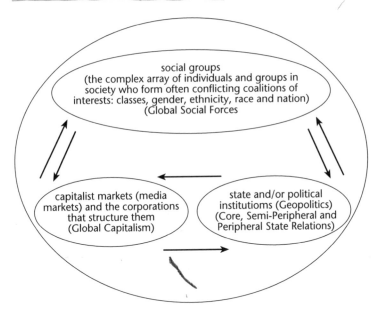

Figure 2.1  A model of global political economy

Figure 2.1 draws attention to the primary sites of social struggle and power in world order, providing us with a structure for understanding world order as a totality within which different structures and agents interact and are related. Analytically they can be seen as separate but related parts of a world order that, as Wallerstein has noted, is an evolving system, that is a system with origins, developments and transformations over time. As Archer has noted, the transformations within a social system are the result of agents acting upon structures with deep historical roots but which are none the less, products of knowledgeable human action (Archer, 1995). Geopolitics and global capitalism provide the underlying conditions within which actors develop their forms of knowledge of the world and subsequently act. Thus, although human agency is free it must always be seen within the objective structural constraints of geopolitics and global capitalism in particular times and places.[5] The three main strands of this model are geopolitics, global capitalism and global social forces. The last General Agreement on Tariffs and Trade (GATT) Round (the Uruguay Round) illustrates the usefulness of this model for understanding developments in the communications industry. As part of the Uruguay Round, the liberalisation of a range of new sectors of the global economy came about largely through the pressure of those political representatives of the leading G7 nations. Included here are not only agreements like so-called trade-related intellectual property rights (TRIPs) but also the liberalisation of media markets themselves, most notably telecommunications. The pressure for this has been growing since the mid-1970s, when major communications corporations, largely American and later European, sought to act collectively to lobby their respective governments to push for these policies (*Third World Resurgence*, 1993, 1995, 1997; Mowlana, 1996: 54–8; Alleyne, 1995; Hamelink, 1994a). A range of political actors resisted these policies across the world, connecting conservative and progressive social forces alike. For conservative social forces in Malaysia, China and Saudi Arabia, for example, liberalisation of the media markets was criticised as being a threat to their cultural autonomy. As a variety of critics have argued, liberalisation is just as plausibly viewed as a potential threat to authoritarian governments who have used their control of the means of communication to protect their power and control their citizens (Tomlinson, 1991; Golding and Harris, 1997; Rothkopf, 1997). Elsewhere, progressive social forces opposed these developments on the grounds that they represented a number of threats to the public, from the erosion of cultural autonomy to the undermining of publicly provided services such as libraries, and to the deepening hegemony of capitalist institutions and private power over public life and democratic politics (Schiller, 1989; Garnham, 1990;

Golding and Murdock, 1991; Philo, 1995; Golding, 1992). In terms of the model in Figure 2.1, we can see that conflicting social forces in global political economy operate at all four levels, all acting in order to shape and influence the policy processes that would determine media markets into the twenty-first century. It comes as little surprise to find that, by and large, the global communication corporations achieved much of what they desired in the final GATT Round (Alleyne, 1995: Chapter 6; Herman and McChesney, 1997: Chapter 1; Elliot and Atkinson, 1998: 252–4). This trend persists in subsequent trade agreements and disputes such as the World Trade Organization and the currently-stalled Multilateral Agreement on Investment (MAI).

The political economy of communications is concerned with giving both an accurate description of the relations of power that persist between these three groups as well as addressing the normative question posed by McDowell that opened this chapter: 'The question is how do we best determine and meet the communication needs of a society?' Such normative questions cannot be avoided in any critical social science and political economy is no exception (Mosco, 1996: Chapter 2). In the remainder of this chapter I want to give an account of two related aspects of the political economy of communication: first, an account of the ongoing political struggles that have led to the changes that have come into being in global communication over the past twenty years; second, how these changes have affected the structure of ownership and control of the global communications industries. To conclude I will tie the significance of these changes to my concern with human security.

## Technology, Ideology and Social Power in the Political Economy of Communication

The development of global communications corporations needs to be understood within the wider context of changes in the global political economy since the mid-1970s. What we have seen since that period has been a movement towards a restructuring of world order within which the power of capital over labour has intensified and been championed by a coalition of the following: internationally minded corporate institutions and actors, elite political actors and institutions, and an array of wider social forces. The collective impact of these transformations has been to impose a range of disciplines upon working people globally (Meiskins, 1998; Gill, 1995). These disciplines have taken diverse forms and their impact reflects a range of factors such as the type of state in question and its social order and culture, its structural location in world order (core, semi-peripheral or peripheral), and the strength of those social groups seeking to resist these changes or proffer alternatives. One example would be Peru under the Fujimori regime, which has utilised military power to impose a form of predatory neoliberal capitalism upon a largely subjugated population. This is not to deny that there has been resistance to these changes within Peruvian society. But Peru illustrates the way in which the structure of political and corporate forces is arrayed against popular resistance (*NACLA*, 1996). Even in a core capitalist state such as Britain where working people have long-established institutions to promote and defend their interests, the 1980s saw a bitter social conflict in which the power of the state was weighed against them. This led to such developments as reactionary legislation to remove various trade union rights; attempts to curb and cut back on public expenditure, which usually targeted the worst-off and most vulnerable in society for the obvious reason that they have the least power to defend themselves; and finally a decline in real wages for a significant section of the working population while at the same time a redistribution of resources to the better-off. The state was supporting a form of capitalism that depended upon dramatically reducing the power of working people to protect themselves either through trade unions or through the law courts (Young, 1989; Pilger, 1992: Part 1; Sivanandan, 1990). Within what has been a global trend towards ever more destructive forms of capitalism, with a few notable exceptions, the communications industries based in the core capitalist states have acted to promote their interests in opening up new markets around the world. Among the *Fortune 500* global businesses there are just two major communications corporations from outside of the core capitalist states: China Telecommunications, appearing for the first time at number 236, and Telefonos De Mexico, which rests at number 482 <http://www.fortune.com/fortune/global500/0,5844,450,00.html>

How and why have the communications industries gone global? Two main factors need to be examined here by way of explanation: new information technology, and the relationship between social power and global communication.

*New Information Technology*

'This is by all odds the most important and lucrative marketplace of the C21.' (US Vice-President Al Gore, in McChesney et al., 1998: 52)

The advent of NIT in the 1970s with breakthroughs in computing and telecommunications technology has been instrumental in the changes to global political economy that we are concerned with. NIT can be seen to comprise all of the following: computers, telecommunications, satellites, cable, computer software, and robotics. Interestingly, a great deal of the technology that comprises the NIT revolution has its origins in publicly funded research and development, often attached to military research. The myth that only a free market can lead to innovation fails to explain the development of such communication breakthroughs as satellite technology, FM radio and the Internet, among others (Herman and McChesney, 1997). Thus it is an alliance of state and corporate actors who have sought to introduce NIT into the workplace and the marketplace as part of the aim of restructuring both state practices and global capitalism. The communications industries have been at the forefront of these developments, moving away from labour-intensive forms of skilled production in core states to production based on the semi-skilled operation of NIT. A range of major social conflicts has ensued in the past two decades, such as the Wapping dispute in the UK where it took the intensive efforts of the state through its police forces to enable News Corporation to succeed in its plans to destroy the print unions that had previously been a major power in Fleet Street (Seymour-Ure, 1997b: 22–3; Negrine, 1996; McNair, 1997: Chapter 7).

As Sivanandan has pointed out, the introduction of NIT has enabled global capitalism to attack the power of working people through redundancies and sackings as a mechanism for increasing profit and controlling the labour force (Sivanandan, 1990: 169–96). Thus NIT innovations of the communications industry have much wider import in the global battle that continues between capital and labour. This, in turn, explains why the communications industry is central to the restructuring of global capital and state formations as we move into the twenty-first century. There is, though, a major contradiction at the heart of these developments of a kind that has arisen throughout the history of capitalism: NIT enables corporations to produce new consumer durables in abundance and at cheaper prices than ever before, whilst at the same time it is also a primary cause of unemployment and declining wages for significant sectors of the world's population that have shaped the global economy since the early 1970s. More goods are being produced while at the same time demand is being curbed. Global economic growth has slowed by roughly half since the mid-1970s, roughly the period when the neoliberal agenda was beginning to take off (Hahnel, 1999: 6). As measured by the gini coefficient,[6] global inequality has increased steadily between core and peripheral states since the mid-1970s (Park and Brat, 1995; and also Brecher et al. 1999).[7] This is an uneven global tendency in terms of its distribution. Hence the early 1990s saw a global economic depression with unprecedented levels of global un- and underemployment while at the same time corporations were recording record profits. The latter were in large part a result of the former (Chomsky, 1994: Part 2). This is not to overlook the sizeable proportion of the world's population who have gained economically from the redistribution of resources from poor to rich over the past twenty years, but it is to emphasise that they remain only a sizeable minority (George, 1994; UNICEF, 2000; World Bank, 1999; Thomas, 2000; UNDP, 1999: Chapters 1 and 5). As the World Bank's report, *World Development Indicators 1999*, notes clearly, the growing gap between rich and poor countries of the world has been a defining feature of the past forty years. Once again we are in the realm of the tyranny of the minority. This is not to deny that globalisation is a complex and contradictory process and structure: it also brings benefits to the developing world, however minimal they may seem in practice. For example, wages paid by transnational corporations (TNCs) to workers in developing countries tend to be higher than those paid elsewhere in the local economy; not much higher, admittedly, but enough to take note of, as Robin Wright has argued (1999).

Four major issues and strands to these breakthroughs in NIT can be seen: digitisation, fibre optics and direct satellite broadcasting, standardisation, and surveillance.

## Digitisation
Digitisation is transforming electronic communication, as old analogue systems are replaced by digital networks. These new systems allow for the production, transmission, reception and storage of information that can be transmitted through a binary code. Consequently the volume and speed of information flows are increased. A logical progression from this, that has caught the imagination of politicians and corporations alike, is the idea of a global superhighway combining digital television, multi-media systems and interactive television. Bill Gates, for one, has referred to this as a shopper's Utopia, while politicians of various ideological persuasions have speculated upon the ways in which digitised communications technology might act to reinvigorate democracy (Dawson and Bellamy Foster, 1998; Poster, 1995; Hague and Loader, 1999; Friedland, 1996; Hacker, 1996).

## Fibre Optics and Direct Satellite Broadcasting
The ocular revolution is part of the infra-structural transformation wrought by NIT and provides the framework for communication between those institutions with the resources needed to take advantage of these developments. Again, it is the major global communications corporations that have been at the forefront of these developments. In conjunction with direct satellite broadcasting (DBS), the ocular system offers greater band width so that more infor-

mation can be carried, and information transmitted as light rather than electronic signals, thus permitting faster flows of information.

DBS can be directed into satellite dishes or via cables and raises important problems for state institutions concerned with controlling the flow of information and communication.

### Standardisation

Standardisation of production is a feature of modern industrial society, and brings the advantage of facilitating smoother flows of information, communication, transport, financial exchanges, and so on. In the communications industry there has been a notable and aggressive push by Microsoft, for example, to monopolise the production and sale of hardware and software on a global scale through its Windows packages. This, in turn, has raised the ire of other capitalists within the communications industries who have pressured the US government into instigating anti-trust actions against Microsoft on the charge of unfair trading practices. Irrespective of the final outcome of the Microsoft case, there is plenty of evidence to suggest that standardisation of technology encourages the convergence of corporations and a movement towards oligopoly in communications markets. As John Malone, former head of US firm Telecommunication International (TCI) (now part of AT & T) has commented on this trend: 'Two or three companies will eventually dominate the delivery of telecommunication services over the information superhighways world-wide. The big bubbles get bigger and the little bubbles disappear' (Dawson and Bellamy Foster, 1998: 54).

### Surveillance

The political economic impact of NIT is wide-ranging and nowhere more so than in the question of surveillance. Corporations are able to utilise computer and telecommunications technology to organise what is euphemistically referred to as 'flexible' production which responds more directly to changing patterns of demand. In practical terms, flexible production means not only more efficient responses to consumer demands but greater discipline over a workforce forced to submit to terms and conditions that erode their general strength in the workplace. The former has been taken to new levels in many markets, with the targeting of particular income groups a speciality. A number of companies have arisen that specialise in selling information about potential consumers so that corporations can target their marketing strategies more directly than ever. In the United States, the Claritas Corporation, for example, has a database of over 500 million individual consumers (Poster, 1995: 89).

Equally, states have sought to utilise NIT for surveillance purposes and the growth of new forms of surveillance of civil populations by state authorities has raised a number of concerns for civil liberties groups around the world. In Europe, for example, there has been a massive expansion of closed circuit television networks (CCTV) with a view to combating city-centre crime. However, as many have been quick to point out, this technology has other potentials, including allowing the state to monitor more closely than ever before the activities of political groups and new social movements (Norris et al., 1998).

Important as NIT undoubtedly is to the transformation of global capitalism and state formations, it needs to be understood in the context of the structure(s) of power between the major political economic actors that I set out earlier in my political economy model. It is to these questions of social power that we must now turn.

## Social Power and Global Communication

NIT is not introduced into society as a neutral tool and, despite the fatalistic tendencies that can be read into many writings on global-isation, we should not fall into the trap of technological determinism – the assumption that social change is an effect of technology. As I mentioned at the beginning of this book, the idea of global communication is more complex than might at first appear to be the case and raises fundamental questions about inequalities of social power in world order. Using Mann's typology of social power is informative here as it provides a framework for the four main currents that have underpinned the ongoing developments in global communication (Mann, 1986). Although I am addressing these different levels of social power in turn, this should not be misconstrued as implying that in practice they are discrete realms of activity. On the contrary, a political-economy analysis recognises the interconnectedness of these processes as part of world order. It also recognises that the world is a lot messier than our models suggest! I have separated them here for heuristic reasons and to clarify a range of key issues that are raised as a consequence.

## Military Power

Military research and development has long been at the forefront of communications technology as states have sought ever more elaborate systems of command and control in preparation for and during conflict. Ongoing developments in global communication are no exception and the power of communication and information technology is now explicitly recognised by senior military and political figures alike. Clinton adviser and academic Professor Joseph Nye, and Admiral William Owens, have written an important article setting out the US's hegemonic position as the world's foremost information superpower and the advantage that this is perceived to give the US in terms of both geopolitics and global political economy (Nye and Owens, 1992). Equally, communications and information technology have always been an important part of military strategy, whether it is through the use of propaganda against domestic or enemy audiences or in terms of the construction and running of defence systems (Jackall, 1995).

The 1960s and 1970s saw an intensification of military research into NIT that ultimately led to many developments that have been taken on by private global communication corporations, for example, the Internet. Originally planned as part of the Pentagon's military strategy to ensure communications in the event of a nuclear conflict, the Internet has subsequently become a staggeringly successful commercial and social arena (Slevin, 2000). It is already the worlds largest single market and this in itself has implications for its future development as either an arena of open debate and communication or as a largely commercialised shopping system. Thus military institutions and interests have played a crucial part of the development of NIT in the past two decades. The US defence initiatives known as Star Wars (SDI) – also known as nuclear missile defence (NMD) – can be seen as part of this process of attempting to legitimise public subsidies for private profit.

### Political Power

States and governments of the core capitalist states[8] have also played a crucial role in the development of global media markets. Apart from the massive public investment in NIT directed through state research funding, tax breaks, investment incentives and so on, the governments of the G7 countries have been pivotal in pushing through the policies at a regional and global level that enables their communication corporations to take advantage of new market opportunities. As W.H. Melody has noted, in practice this leads to an increasing concentration of market power in the hands of fewer corporations – essentially something like a global oligopoly (Melody, 1994). Ben Bagdikian has supported this claim noting that in the period between 1983 and the early 1990s the number of major media companies had declined from fifty to less than twenty due to mergers in the industry, a trend that shows no sign of decreasing (Bagdikian, 1992: 21). The actions of these governing authorities and states have been important in offering some kind of legitimacy to these changes in global political economy generally and the communications markets in particular precisely because they carry a democratic mandate. The importance of these changes is that they help to sustain an attack upon the principles of publicly provided services whilst at the same time they help to underpin the idea of public subsidy for private profit and power. Taking the

European Union as an example, where once the BBC and its model of public service broadcasting, however flawed, were seen as something of a blueprint for nationally based broadcasting, but the 1980s saw a shift of power and ideas within the European Union. From 1980 onwards and with the advent of Berlusconi's private multi-channel network in Italy, the policy emphasis in the European Community shifted towards 'consumer sovereignty', choice and the commercial possibilities opened up for multi-channel broadcasting (Tunstall and Palmer, 1991: Chapters 2, 4 and 7). There is little reason to doubt that so far it is this latter model of privately owned and controlled commercial broadcasting that has prevailed, not just regionally but now increasingly globally, as I will illustrate later in this chapter. This raises questions concerning the contradictions between private power and public interest that are significant for human security and its concern with the autonomy of citizens – I examine this issue in Chapter 3.

*Economic Power*

In terms of economic power the major actors pushing for the liberalisation of the communications industries were unsurprisingly based in the core capitalist states. If initially in the mid-1970s it was the US communications corporations that were pushing the ideological agenda that I will turn to shortly, they were joined in the early 1980s by an important bloc of European corporations (Boyd-Barrett, 1997). As a group these communications corporations had reached saturation point in their domestic markets and saw the potential to expand into new markets with a new range of consumer goods which included videos, personal computers and satellite broadcasting. Thus corporate groups lobbied political institutions at both national and regional levels, encouraging their political representatives to push these issues into international fora, most noticeably through the GATT Rounds and subsequently the WTO (Mowlana, 1996: 45; Hamelink, 1994a; WTO, 1997). The importance of the communications corporations to the transformation of global capitalism cannot be underestimated. The technology developed and sold by the industries has proven to be pivotal in the reorganisation of production and working practices and has been a key factor in the attempt by capital to curb the organisation and power of working people to protect themselves from private power.

*Ideological Power*

'The world's political structures are completely obsolete ... the critical issue of our time is the conceptual conflict between the global optimisation of resources and the independence of

nation-states.' (Jacques Maison Rouge, former Chief Officer of
European Operations, IBM, in Mulgan, 1991: 220)

This quote from Maison Rouge is indicative of the powerful ambitions
of neoliberal political economy that have been instrumental in the
development of what is now commonly referred to as economic globalisation (Held et al., 1999; Dicken, 1998). Contrary to the views of
those who see these trends as part of the inevitable withering away of
the state in the face of the demands of global capital movements,
Maison Rouge's quote reveals that the goals of neoliberal political
economy are more complex than this. Rather, it is an attempt to
*restructure the relationship between states, capitalist markets and social
groups*, with states generally being expected to take on a range of tasks
that primarily support and enhance the position of market actors as
opposed to intervening in the economy for wider reasons of public
interest or need. In the next section I will set out what I take to be the
main ideological principles of neoliberal political economy and how
they have offered support to what is termed 'economic globalisation'
before turning to the reasons why they present problems for human
security. I want to begin with an overview of the three strands of
neoliberal political economy that have underpinned global economic
changes at the four levels of world order.

## Neoliberal Political Economy

### Liberalisation

The movement towards a global economic order based upon free
trade has been a rhetorical ambition of major capitalist institutions
in the West since the end of the Second World War. The General
Agreement on Tariffs and Trade (GATT) was established on the basis
of promoting freer trade over a period of time; its successor, the
more powerful World Trade Organization (WTO) has even more
weaponry to enforce these principles (Seabright, 2000; Shiva, 1999;
Mokhiber and Weissman, 1999; Luthens, 1999; George, 2000). The
world economy has been transformed in a number of significant
ways since the breakdown of the Bretton Woods system began in
1971 (Spero, 1990: 41–8). In neoliberal terms, free trade promotes
market efficiency, competition and the maximisation of resource
allocation in terms of supply and demand reaching a natural equilibrium. The developments in global communication are part of the
ambition of (ideally) perfecting market transactions in a situation
where, in theory, consumers can make rational choices on the basis
of perfect information. Bill Gates, for example, has speculated as to
this possibility in his chapter on 'Friction Free Capitalism' in his
book *The Road Ahead* (1995).

*Privatisation*

As part of the drive to promote an enhanced role for the market in the global economy, states have either willingly sought or been encouraged by agencies such as the international financial institutions (IFIs), most notably but not exclusively the World Bank and the International Monetary Fund (IMF), to sell off publicly held assets to private actors and institutions. The assumption here is that publicly owned resources lack the dynamism and entrepreneurial spirit of the private sector. Although privatisation is a complex process that takes many forms according to the political institutions and culture of distinct nation-states, the principle is itself reasonably straightforward (Feigenbaum and Henig, 1997; Berg and Berg, 1997; Ricupero, 1997). From the perspective of neoliberal political economy, the private sector takes risks and innovates in search of reward while the public sector has a tendency to promote dependency and ultimately complacency and inefficiency (Merrien, 1998; *Journal of International Affairs*, 1997).

*Deregulation*
A logical outcome of these ideas is that states should aim to remove the excessive regulatory burden upon private companies as this inhibits their innovation, flexibility and entrepreneurial spirit. State regulation is often seen as a largely self-serving process which helps to legitimise and reinforce the authority of state institutions while doing little to enable people to take advantage of their natural capacities to succeed in a capitalist market economy (Hayek, 1944). Changes in technology and consumer demand, coupled with the expanded production capacity of major corporations over the past twenty-five years for neoliberals, means that there is less need for the state to intervene in markets on behalf of the public, as in a free market goods that do not come up to standard will fail to sell as there are an increasing number of alternatives on offer. It is not in the financial self-interest of companies to produce goods that do not satisfy consumer demand as ultimately they will lose out. The dramatic changes in the communications markets over the past twenty years with a proliferation of new consumer goods is a classic example of this argument. Thus, for the neoliberal there is a clear case for self-regulating markets.

## The Impact of Neoliberal Political Economy – Globalising Tendencies

Taken together, these three principles central to the neoliberal vision set out by Maison Rouge seek to fundamentally alter the structure(s) of power in the relationship between states, capitalist markets and social groups. In terms of its impact on world order, we can see a number of significant tendencies emerging.

## Global Capital Accumulation

The main mechanism driving neoliberal political economy at the global level is the continuing integration of capitalism as a system in which capital accumulation is increasingly taking place on a global rather than on a national scale (Drache, 1996: 31–61). As has long been argued, it is transnational corporations and IFIs that are the primary agents for this restructuring of the global economy, as private institutions increasingly take control of investment and trade (Burchill, 1996b: 50–63; Dicken, 1992: 1, 48–50). In effect, this transformation of the world economy has been developing rapidly since the decline of the Bretton Woods system in the early 1970s and has been amplified by the liberalising economic changes since then. The collective power of these transnational capitalist institutions to set the global political economic agenda represents the most important tendency in economic globalisation in the past twenty years. Various writers have correctly noted that globalisation, when understood as the movement towards an integrated capitalist world order, has been an inherent feature of modernity (Hirst and Thompson, 1996); but I would argue that it is only with recent developments in communications technology that the full complexity of this process has begun to take shape in terms of the dramatically enhanced speed, flow and volume of capital transactions (Held et al., 1999: Chapter 4 in particular). In addition to the power that accrues from the control of capital and existing in complex relationship to it comes an accumulation of other forms of power that are part of the hierarchical structure of social power in world order: for example, power over information, power over regulation of trade and investment, and finally the accumulation of military power (Thomas and Wilkin, 1997; Gill and Law, 1990).

## Global Patterns of Social Power, Exploitation and Hierarchy

Directly related to the movement from forms of national capital accumulation to those that are increasingly taking place on a global scale are the widening forms of social and economic inequality and exploitation that are a defining feature of world order. As TNCs utilise the access that a 'liberalised' world economy brings to their capacity to seek out the most profitable forms of investment and locations for production, so we are witnessing a substantive global social restructuring (Raghavan, 1990; Amin 1997; Cox, 1989: 46).[9] This sees the movement of manufacturing industries from traditional Northern locations to a number of key Southern regions.[10] At

the same time, there has been a steady transformation in the older
industrial areas to new forms of production and accumulation. The
social consequences of these changes have led to starkly uneven
forms of development. In the traditionally rich Northern states,
forms of social deprivation, poverty and ill-health have re-emerged
with a vengeance alongside areas of comparative wealth and general
affluence (Chomsky, 1993: Chapter 11; World Bank, 1999 and
2000[11]). While the South is still the overwhelming site of absolute
poverty in the world, there has been a significant redistribution of
resources not only from South to North in geographic terms, but
from poor-to-rich in global terms (Brown and Kane, 1995: 46;
Brittain and Elliot, 1996; Keegan, 1996). This presents a far more
complex picture of inequality in world order and these transformations are perhaps most clearly illustrated in the development of
global cities. Cities throughout the world are expanding to incorporate historically unprecedented waves of migration from rural areas
to urban in search of work opportunities; as a result urban poverty
increases alongside the astonishing architectural and financial
wealth. The latter are the ultimate symbols of the nodes of political,
economic and cultural power that are today's global cities (Castles
and Miller, 1993; Jameson, 1991; Walker, 1995: 42–7; Sassen, 1991).
The combined impact of mass unemployment, migration and
economic retrenchment portends, as many are noting, social
problems of unparalleled proportions (*Third World Resurgence*, 1994;
Cox, 1989: 47; Wallace and Bradshaw, 1996.). Thus, the patterns of
inequality that are developing are best understood as complex and
integrated features of the four levels of world order as opposed to
patterns that are seen as features of the relations between discrete
nation-states. Figure 2.2, from the World Bank's *World Development
Indicators Report* for 1999, illustrates the ever widening gap in global
inequality as measured in terms of GNP and GNP per capita.

*Private Power over Human Need*

The third and related impact of neoliberal ideology that I emphasise
here is the transcendence of private power over large areas of social,
economic and political life (Schiller, 1989). The ideas and values associated with contemporary neoliberal political economy have gained
international ascendancy in the past two decades through the
increasing confidence of major political and economic actors to
promote and defend them. They have been able to support the
authority of private actors and institutions to control the direction
that economic policy takes, from the national level through to the
workings of the IFIs (Bienefeld, 1996: 415–44). When coupled with
the impact of world-wide political movements towards liberalised
trade, privatised economies and deregulation of state controls, these

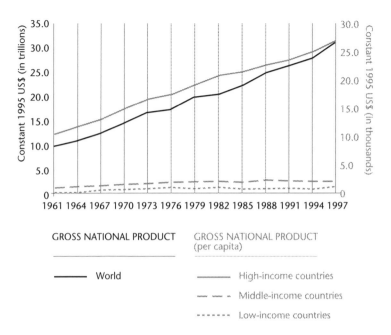

**Figure 2.2 The growing gap between rich and poor countries**

*Source*: World Bank, 1999.

neoliberal values and ideas have taken on the form of a new global common sense, at an elite level at least (Gill, 1990). In effect, there is a dominant ideology that has served to unite the interests of a range of powerful political and economic elites under the guise of providing a universal blueprint for progress and development. While there are functional aspects to this ideology (for example, it helps to legitimise the power of private capitalist interests over those of both the workforce and those excluded from work), it is far from being all embracing. I will illustrate later that this ideology is part of an ongoing struggle for control over the direction that social, political and economic organisation will take in the early twenty-first century. Diverse social forces have sought to resist this neoliberal transformation and they, too, are of great significance for an understanding of human security as I will illustrate in Chapter 6 (Brecher et al., 1993).

*The Changing Role, Power and Autonomy of States*

A common theme in globalisation literature, and one that echoes Maison Rouge's concern, is that both the sovereignty and autonomy of nation-states have been seriously diminished by the movement towards a globalised economy (Reich, 1992). No single nation-state is said to be able to resist the power of continually transforming patterns of global investment and the relocation of capital, as private investors seek out the most efficient and profitable locations. Indeed, this belief is an important strand of the current hegemony of neoliberal political economy and has found widespread acceptance among political parties of all persuasions (Gray, 1998). While I do not seek to deny the power of the increased mobility and volatility of capitalist transactions, equally I do not subscribe to the view that there has been a general levelling down of the power of nation-states. Rather, what needs to be emphasised is that changes in the sovereignty and autonomy of nation-states is *differentially* distributed in the world order. For example, major economies such as those of Eastern Europe, South East and East Asia or Mexico are either directly or indirectly organised under the auspices of representatives of the IFIs (Gowan, 1998). However, the core capitalist states remain firmly on top of the hierarchical power structure(s) of world order, as is illustrated by the way in which they are able to organise and control the aforementioned IFIs (Chomsky, 1994: 178–88). Indeed, there are strong reasons to suppose that contrary to neoliberal orthodoxy (embodied in what is referred to as the 'Washington Consensus[12]), TNCs actually need nation-states to remain strong and powerful actors in certain respects (Waltz, 1999: 6; Jenkins, 1987: 177). For example, strong nation-states are required to maintain social order and to help discipline populations into both employed and unemployed sectors as well as providing legitimacy for these policy changes. While nation-states may have increasingly retreated from certain forms of economic activity (for example, public welfare), they have expanded their powers in other areas, most generally concerning domestic surveillance, policing and control (Shaw, 1994: 72–9). Nor should we overlook the fact that it is nation-states that have brought about and helped to legitimise the changes to the global political economy that have taken place. A consequence of this has been that the economic role of nation-states has been substantively redrawn towards providing increased financial incentives for private investors to utilise the resources that a nation-state has to offer. This takes the form of a familiar litany of requirements, from tax-free trade zones, general reductions in direct corporate and personal taxation and increases in regressive taxation to reductions in public welfare, and the selling-off of public assets to private investors and corporations. All of this amounts to the *embedding of the principle of public investment for private profit and power on the assumption that it will lead to the maximum utilisation of resources* (Petrella, 1996; Krugman, 1989).[13] My conclusion, then, is that while many nation-states can certainly be said to have seen their 'autonomy' and 'sovereignty' significantly diminished, it is also the case that the core capitalist states have acquired more power in terms of their military capabilities and political authority in world order.[14] These core capitalist states are unsurprisingly familiar and reflect well-entrenched hierarchies of power in world order. The core capitalist states, essentially the G7 bloc led by the US and their representative actors and institutions, are the key here. This is a hierarchical system in which the multiple forms of power (economic, political, military and ideological) help to maintain and stretch these structures of world order over time. The relations of domination that persist and develop in world order are complex, combining local, national, regional and global relations around a range of issues such as class, patriarchy, militarism and ethnicity.

What we are left with as a consequence of this is a world order that is characterised by an increasingly unstable and chaotic form of social and economic organisation (Corbridge et al., 1994; Soros, 1999). There is nothing inevitable or permanent about the forms of social power that structure world order. The factors I have focused upon in this chapter serve to illustrate the ongoing tension between existing social relations of power and the institutional frameworks that regulate them. The uneven impact of the emergence of a global political economy has been exacerbated by the very factors that were once seen as crucial to the revival of a classical political economy: the liberalising and deregulation of finance and markets globally so that efficiency and competition could be maximised for the benefit of the consumer. In practice, this tendency has proven to be far more problematic than neoliberal orthodoxy would predict and has now led to major financial crises on various occasions, for example, the near-total collapse of major stock exchanges such as New York's in 1987 or the rapid and sudden decline of economies that were once held up as models of fiscal rectitude, as illustrated by the ongoing crisis in South East Asia (Chossudovsky, 1997: 9–13).

What we see in practice, then, is a marked mismatch between neoliberal theory and practice. In theory, the neoliberal agenda posits a universal formula that will bring the good society to all in the guise of freedom and rational choice in a global market. In practice, the commitment to free trade on the part of core capitalist states and their corporations is at best specific to particular markets and at worst merely an ideological device used somewhat crudely to cover up a mixture of policies shaped around free trade and protectionism. In some respects there is nothing new about this as anyone familiar with E.H. Carr's classic *The Twenty Years Crisis* (1995) can attest. The powerful core capitalist states and their corporations have sought to impose freer trade in those markets where they are most likely to dominate due to technological advantages, economies of scale and so on. Hence the struggle in the last GATT Round to include new areas such as intellectual property rights (TRIPs) and trade-related investment measures (TRIMs). In areas where developing countries might have an advantage, such as agriculture, trade is far more tightly managed and restricted through a familiar range of non-tariff barriers. In practical terms, the neoliberal political economy agenda provides protection and subsidies for core capitalist states and their companies and free trade for those in the periphery and semi-periphery that cannot compete (Watkins, 1999). What the neoliberal model fails to address is that in practice social, economic and political life are not simply shaped by rational actors seeking to perfect market efficiency. On the contrary, they are shaped by expressions of social power and interest that in turn reflect factors such as class, patriarchy and nationalism. It is social power that is missing from the neoliberal model of political economy and it is power that must be central to a critical analysis of its implications for human security. There is little reason to doubt, I think, that neoliberal political economy represents a major threat to human security in the areas of need satisfaction and human autonomy and for reasons which I will turn to later in this book.

## A Qualitative Change in Global Communication?

In this chapter I have set out the political economy context in which changes in the communications industries have taken place over the past three decades. Clearly they must be rooted in the context of a wider concern with the structure(s) of power between states, capitalist markets and social groups as I set out in my model earlier in the chapter. We can see then that a powerful and fluid coalition of elites that cuts across political, economic, cultural and military institutions has formed and has been able to push through policy changes that have served to enhance the position of capital over that of working and non-working people (Gill, 1995; Van Der Pijl, 1998). This, in turn, has also served to help restructure state practices in the direction of shifting resources from a public arena to the control of private power. This latter point also means the attempt to limit and roll back the redistribution of resources from rich to poor wherever possible, and increasingly takes decisions over the control of resources out of the hands of democratic institutions and into those of unaccountable private ones. For these reasons, it is plausible to argue that what has occurred represents not just a quantitative shift in global order but increasingly a qualitative one. With more commodities being produced and distributed more widely than ever before, with a privileged section of the world's population able to take advantage of new opportunities for movement, investment, financial, and political gain, world order has been transformed in terms of the structure(s) of power between these conflicting social forces. More abstractly but just as significantly, questions of social time and space have also been qualitatively changed. Where once technology and geography imposed important constraints upon political economy the NIT that I have focused upon in this section has helped to transform the global political economy by enhancing the surveillance and investment power of capital and its ability to divide and discipline working people (Hewson, 1994). To a significant extent, capital has freed itself of the need of any *particular* nationally based form of labour. Increasingly, it has the capacity to pick and choose between the relative skills of nationally based labour, playing them off against each other as it seeks out the best return on its investment. The developing trade between the US, Canada and Mexico since the ratification of the North Atlantic Free Trade Association (NAFTA) agreement in 1994 illustrates the ability of capital to divide labour against itself. This agreement has enabled major TNCs to seek out cheaper labour as a means of controlling wage costs and at the same time undermining both the solidarity of working people and the pay and conditions that they endure. At times the tactics used by companies in the US to intimidate their workforces into 'renegotiating' their terms of work have been brutally crude (Chomsky, 1997).[15] This represents a chronic weakening of the ability of working people to defend themselves from powerful private interests. This trend is not irreversible or one that cannot be challenged by working people, but it seems clear that any adequate response by labour will have to be transnational rather than nationally based. At the same time, the military power of core capitalist states such as the US and the UK has dramatically increased, usually under the cover of the UN or NATO, to impose their conception of geopolitical order upon the world as we have seen in the 1990s.[16] Equally, as I will illustrate in Chapter 6, these developments also offer important potentials for those social groups opposed to the imposition of private power and state authority over working and non-working people. The latter is a complex, developing and as yet emergent factor of global civil society whose activities are in significant part structured through communications technology. What I want to do now is turn to the transformed structures of ownership and control of the global communications corporations in order to clarify why this represents a qualitative shift in the balance of power in global order.

## Global Communications? The Changing Structure of the Communications Industries

The past two decades have seen a series of significant developments in the structure of the communications industries that reflect the themes that were addressed in the previous section. A conjunction of technological developments married with changing political ideologies in the core capitalist states and backed, crucially, by a bloc of corporate and political elites all coalesced to help bring about these changes. The part played by NIT in this process of global economic restructuring has been pivotal and has helped to fuel ideas about the possible perfecting of capitalist markets coupled with a qualitative change in social relations. The latter is said to see the world moving beyond old divisions of class, gender and race towards what is often described as the 'information society'. I will turn to the latter theme more fully in Chapters 4 and 5 as it is a key issue for human security and global communication, but suffice to say for the moment that the neoliberal model of the information society is one in which ordinary citizens are said to be empowered at the expense of states and companies. This is to be achieved through increased access to new and unprecedented volumes and forms of information from which they can exercise their critical and rational scrutiny of powerful institutions. In the information society, there is nowhere to hide for those who would seek to abuse their power and authority (Habermas, 1999: 1–2).[17] This idea ties in with the revived interest in civil society that is reflected in a great deal of contemporary political analysis and rhetoric. Both former President Clinton and former Vice-President Gore have talked about the positive political virtues generated through the extended use of NIT in democratic processes (Hacker, 1996). In civil society, ordinary citizens exercise their liberties and form voluntary groups or act as individuals in pursuit of their particular interests. In this respect, civil society is the realm of plurality in neoliberal thought, in which no single group, actor or institution can dominate the majority. This structure of power between public and private actors is a classic liberal theme, of course, and what is important about developments in the communications industry and NIT is the way that they offer an *apparent* endorsement of this model of a world order in which power is increasingly dispersed among different groups and bodies.[18] In order to make sense of these developments, I want to set out the changing structure of ownership and control in global communication before turning to the neoliberal justification and defence of these tendencies. In the remaining chapters of this book I will be elaborating a critique of this neoliberal justification in the context of the implications for human security of these changing patterns of ownership and control.

## Global Communication and the Changing Structure of Ownership and Control – From Synergy to Oligopoly

Ongoing developments in the communications industry are seen by many as unprecedented transformations. The past twenty years have seen a wave of mergers taking place in the communications markets that has seen successful companies joining together in an effort to increase their power in the media markets. Thus a range of companies have merged under the guise of 'synergy', the pooling of centres of excellence as a means to improve market transactions and service provision, leading to new communication institutions, including, for example, Time-Warner and Disney (incorporating Capital Cities/ABC). Similar developments have been taking place in the field of telecommunications with attempts by BT, ACC, AT & T and others to become one of the three 'bubbles' that John Malone described as the logical outcome of mergers in the telecommunications market. The logic behind this trend is straightforward when viewed in terms of neoliberal political economy: companies that have concentrated their efforts in different areas of the communications markets come together in order to pool their techniques and resources. This form of merger sees communications companies integrating horizontally, that is, connecting with other companies in the same industry. Taking this tendency further still, we find communications companies also linking themselves with other industrial concerns, in a process known as vertical integration. General Electric is a good example, with its diverse industrial interests including its media holdings in NBC. General Electric brought RCA in 1986 and with it NBC news. This enabled GE to combine media power with its other industrial, financial and political interests. GE remains a major recipient of US government defence contracts worth $40 billion per annum (Bagdikian, 1992: 11). Such a relationship raises clear issues of a conflict of interest between General Electric's media operations and its armaments interests. How critical and independent of government can such an institution afford to be in its media coverage if it is at the same time eating from the trough of public subsidy?

As the communications corporations have grown in size and global reach, they have transformed their market strategies to think in terms of global market reach as opposed to national targets. A good example of this has been the meteoric rise of News Corporation since the early 1970s. Through a series of aggressive and often risky business activities, Rupert Murdoch's media power has extended to all parts of the globe until he is now in a situation where News Corporation embraces nine different media in six continents (Herman and McChesney, 1997: 72). As the power of these corporations has grown, they have been able to take advantage of their vast resources to pressurise national governments into pursuing policies that are sensitive to their particular interests: low taxation, self-regulation, liberalisation and privatisation of publicly controlled communications corporations. This new common-sense ideology has been sharply illustrated in British political culture over the past two decades as the Labour Party has sought to distance itself from its socialist history in favour of a variant of neoliberal policies (Ramsay, 1998; Elliot and Atkinson, 1998: Chapters 4–7). The politician's fear of 'media moguls' is not a new factor in modern politics as we saw in the Introduction, and can be traced back to the early years of the twentieth century in the writings of those like Walter Lippmann who observed:

> The significant revolution of modern times is not industrial or economic or political, but the revolution takes place in the art of creating consent among the governed ... within the life of the new generation now in control of affairs, persuasion has become a self-conscious art and a regular organ of popular government. None of us begins to understand the consequences, but it is no daring prophecy to say that the knowledge of how to create consent will alter every political practice. [McNair, 1995: opening statement]

Similarly, Stephen Koss has written on the fear of the so-called 'press barons' exhibited by British governments in the course of the twentieth century – the fears expressed are pervasive in democratic and undemocratic societies alike (Koss, 1990). The communications industries have the potential power of influence over a mass audience that raises great fears for political actors who might find themselves on the wrong side of the communications companies (Jamieson, 1992 and 1997).[19] In practical terms this has led to a situation over the past twenty years where the major national governments in the global economy have come under pressure to promote policies of economic restructuring that reflect the interests of not only communications companies but of major capitalist institutions in general. Political parties and social groups resistant to untrammelled capitalist markets or proposing alternative strategies connect across a wide range of political thought but there is little reason to doubt that they have suffered collectively in this struggle. As global markets have indeed been transformed along the lines set out earlier, reflecting the interests of powerful capitalist institutions, they have tended to undermine the power of working and non-working people to defend themselves and their interests. These tendencies in the communications markets must be viewed as part of the wider changing political economy of global capitalism as it seeks to incorporate the technological developments offered by NIT as a means for restructuring production and working practices generally. Within communications markets, this emerging political economy has led to a narrowing of ownership and control of the major institutions, which are often referred to as the 'agenda-setting media'; I will illustrate this in the next chapter when I consider the global flow of communication. What we are witnessing in practice is a movement towards a global communications industry in which a limited number of corporations come to dominate the production of goods and services: an oligopoly in which there is competition between a handful of transnational corporations. This has serious implications for human security and its concern with autonomy and the remainder of this book will draw out these issues in stark detail. I want now to turn to the grounds offered in neoliberal political economy to justify these developments.

## Globalisation and the Information Society: an introduction

In neoliberal political economy, the benefits of globalisation and the transformation of both the global economy in general and of the communications industries in particular are part and parcel of what is taken to be 'the information society' (*Economist*, 2000i). The justifications and explanations of these changes offered in neoliberal political economy are far-ranging and have proven to possess a durability in the policies of international financial institutions such as the IMF and the World Bank. My intention here is only to introduce the neoliberal idea of the information society. I will turn to it in more detail in Chapters 4 and 5. The alleged benefits of the information society can be seen as:

- The perfecting of market transactions
- The expansion of global markets
- The restructuring of the workplace
- The commodification of information
- The revival of democracy.

A prevailing theme among neoliberal views of globalisation is that the globalisation of capitalism in its neoliberal form is the only progressive game in town (*Economist*, 2000b). As before, the issue that remains central here for human security concerns social power among individuals and classes in any given social order. Do all citizens gain from these developments? Do they all gain equally? Does this inequality matter? Who is excluded from these benefits, and why? My contention here is that in effect the political economy changes introduced by NIT, however contradictory, ultimately serve thus far to reinforce existing patterns of hierarchy and inequality. Unless subordinate social groups are able to resist this and transform the way that they are introduced into society, it is difficult to see how any other conclusion could be reached.

Part of the task of reviving democracy for neoliberal ideology has been to promote and reinvigorate the meaning and practices of civil society. The age of the entrepreneur is indeed the age of civil society, for neoliberals a realm where private citizens pursue their private interests with minimal interference by the state (Ohmae, 1990). The net result is said to be that these private actions will generate public goods. The 'risk society' encourages innovation and ambition and offers financial reward as its ultimate goal. The communications industries have been at the forefront of this particular revival of civil society. Media figures such as Rupert Murdoch and Ted Turner have set out a business philosophy that combines innovations and reward with a political agenda that promotes liberty and independence (Murdoch, 1994 and 1995). As Turner has said:

> No group of people has a greater responsibility or a greater opportunity to change these ways of doing things than the people here in the television and communications business. All of us have a tremendous social responsibility to our nation and to the people and all the creatures on this planet to programme at least part of our own networks with information that will create a sense of brotherhood and global citizenship. [Turner, 1994: 42]

Ultimately we are left with a political economy that has a clear conception of 'the good life', the means by which society can be best organised for the interests of all citizens. In neoliberal terms this is constituted by a 'market society',[20] where individual liberty is maximised and in which consumers and citizens alike are able to exercise their freedoms to make rational choices about the things that affect them. What I will show as this book progresses are the weaknesses in this model and the ways in which it contradicts the goals of human security. For the neoliberal political economy, life is a competition in which there are winners and losers. *The ethos for human security must be that nobody wins unless everybody wins.*

## Conclusions: Problems for Human Security

If human security is concerned with the realisation of human need and autonomy, then it is clear that the role of what are increasingly becoming global communications corporations are pivotal to these matters. The combined impact of global communications upon human security is felt in two ways. The first way is through the role that NIT has played in the restructuring of global social relations, for example, as seen in changing forms of economic decision making and work practices, and also in the changing structures and practices of political institutions. Second, the increasing concentration of patterns of ownership and control of the communications industry raises important questions for human autonomy that need to be given due consideration. The remainder of this book is concerned with both of these issues.

## CHAPTER 3

# Human Security and Global Communication – Into the Twenty-First Century

Knowledge itself is power. (Francis Bacon)[1]

Truth is linked in circular fashion with systems of power which produce and sustain it, and to effects of power which it induces and which extend it. A 'regime' of truth. (Michel Foucault, 1980: 33)

## Knowledge, Power and Rationality

As I mentioned in Chapter 1, the debate surrounding human security cannot be understood without recognising that it is part of ongoing discussions in social and political theory about notions of the good society. By this I mean the contrasting ideas about how we should organise our social, political and economic systems so as to maximise what we take to be the most important human values. Of course, this latter theme is itself a deeply contested issue and often hinges around debates about individual liberty and the common good (Plant, 1991). This is not a book that aspires to enter directly into those debates but what must be set out here is that the concept of human security has clear implications for these questions. Abstract social and political theory that fails to connect *descriptive* and *explanatory* analysis (what is the case and why) and *prescriptive* analysis (what could or should be the case) can often lead to sterile debates that serve largely to stimulate the academic community but invariably fail to connect with a wider audience (Fay, 1975). Important though such works may be in their own right, my intention here is to examine the ways in which a descriptive and explanatory analysis of global communications patterns and prevailing tendencies feeds into prescriptive debates about the good society. As colleagues in the largely Anglo-American analytic tradition of philosophy never tire of explaining, these are not deductive conclusions. None the less, it is a prescriptive analysis that makes non-demonstrative inferences and which attempts to ground them in an analysis of existing social relations. We can and must argue about the conclusions that can be drawn from them, recognising the fallibility of our claims.

The two quotations that I began this chapter with are important for my account of human security precisely because they reflect contrasting poles of thought about the role that knowledge plays in the evolution of human affairs.[2] Human security is concerned with issues of global emancipation rather than focusing upon the emancipation of people within a particular state or nation, in an attempt to make sense of the interrelated history of the modern world order (Wallerstein, 1999). Ultimately, human security is *global* human security. As such, it is part of the modernist tradition of social and political thought that has sought to emphasise the need for social justice, most commonly recognised today in the discourse of human rights and needs. The problems with claims about universal normative principles are well recognised and form a major part of contemporary social and political theory (Squires, 1993). The quote from Foucault reflects a powerful critique of such aspirations, as it implies that ideas about universal norms are in truth always particular ideas, emerging in a certain time and place and at the expense of alternate understandings of what is the most just social arrangement. These ideas are not and cannot be universal principles by which we could seek to organise politics, economy and society.

The debate between postmodernism and what is seen as the Enlightenment tradition of social and political thought often revolves around the twin poles of universalism and particularism. By this I mean that claims to knowledge (in this case, knowledge of what constitutes social justice) are presented as being either universal truths; or else they are seen as being thoroughly particular, reflecting the values of a particular discourse at a particular time and place. These contrasting positions frequently recur in social and political theory as representing the respective positions of Enlightenment and postmodern thought (Rorty, 1989; Macintyre, 1987; Connolly, 1989). I want briefly to set out here the way in which human security might be seen to draw from the Enlightenment tradition of social and political thought and its concern with universal grounds for social justice. It is important that proponents of human security are able to set out the theoretical assumptions that underpin their work and in so doing I will illustrate that human security does not eschew the Enlightenment ideas of truth, progress and social justice. The latter themes have come under severe and critical scrutiny in contemporary social and political theory for a variety of reasons already alluded to. It is important for human security and its concerns with global emancipation that it has both the theoretical and empirical grounds for defending its views against the various forms of anti-rationalism and judgmental relativism[3] that are prevalent themes in social and political thought. For example, in international relations the idea of a 'national interest', the guiding principle for foreign policy analysis and military security, is built upon the assumption that interests are relative or particular to distinct groups of people as nations. As such there can be no higher or universal interests that override this.

This relativist argument has had disastrous implications for global geopolitics in the history of the modern state system, pitching groups of people against each other often on the basis of crude and propagandistic assumptions about inherent or inalienable differences that render them as predetermined enemies, rivals or friends. Thus at the beginning of the Second World War, the Russian people in general and Stalin in particular quickly became the 'friends' of Britain and the US where previously they had been official enemies. In the immediate postwar period they very quickly and consciously became 'natural' enemies again as the geopolitical and economic ambitions of the US and British ruling elites changed. These changes of strategy were mirrored by attempts to transform popular consciousness in the US and the UK against the Soviet Union, communism and socialism. The propaganda efforts cut across both popular culture *and* political culture (Macdonald, 1985; Jackall, 1995; Fones-Wolf, 1994; Blum, 1986; Carey, 1997; Saunders, 2000). If we reject this kind of nationalist relativism in favour of defending a universal basis to human security, then how can we escape from the danger of what we might call 'epistemological imperialism'? By this I mean a theme that E.H. Carr analysed in *The Twenty Years Crisis* (1995), the idea that in any given era what we define as good, right and the best is simply a reflection of the interests of ruling elites. As such it is a product of dominant and oppressive social power rather than a reflection of social justice. Not only can this be resisted but it is vital for human security analyses that it is and I think that the following grounds are adequate for our purposes.

There are two parts – ontological and epistemological – to my response to the criticisms levelled by various forms of anti-rationalist social and political thought with regard to the idea of human security as a universal goal. Taking the ontological issue first, human needs are central to human security and they provide the common feature of human nature that enables us to set out and defend a coherent account of human security in universalist terms. Human needs are both universal *and* particular in the sense that while we share with each other such universal needs as the need for food, drink, culture and so on, the particular forms that they take will reflect a host of individual and social factors. For example, I need food but I do not need walnuts or almonds because I am allergic to them. Likewise, I do not eat meat as it contradicts my

religious beliefs. None the less, I still need food of *some kind*. Hence
it is both a universal and a particular need. The good society will be
one that takes account of the complexity of human needs in both
their universal and particular manifestations. In order to make
sense of this and to decide what arrangements are best suited for
realising this goal we also need autonomy, the second major strand
of human security. By autonomy I am building upon the idea laid
down by Doyal and Gough who argue that being autonomous
means (ideally) being able to make free, uncoerced and rational
choices about such matters. As they argue: 'Since physical survival
and personal autonomy are the preconditions for any individual
human action in any culture, they constitute the most basic human
needs – those which must be satisfied to some degree before actors
can effectively participate in their form of life to achieve any other
valued goals' (Doyal and Gough, 1991: 54). Thus Doyal and Gough
set out an important benchmark for human security when they
note that substantive autonomy (what they call critical autonomy)
requires both freedom of agency for individuals as well as the political freedoms necessary in order to take part in the processes of
decision making that structure any social and political system. The
importance of global communication is transparent here, in terms
of the media, NIT and education. If we are to attain human security,
then it will be a social order, a good life, established ultimately on
the basis of a solidarity in which we are able to participate meaningfully in the decisions that affect our lives. In order to be
meaningful participants in such a world order, we need not only to
have our human needs satisfied but also to have the autonomy
necessary to enable us to make rational and uncoerced judgements
about our world (Habermas, 1989). This is an ideal, of course, as
critics will no doubt charge and in practice we will always be prone
to errors and mistakes. But as a guide towards which human
security might aim, the onus surely lies upon its opponents or
critics to elaborate upon alternative procedures and structures for
human emancipation.

Turning to the second area of my defence against irrationalism
or anti-rationalist critics of human security, I want to address the
epistemological assumptions underpinning the approach. In terms
of our epistemological claims about human security it is important
that we recognise our limitations. By this I mean quite simply that
we recognise our fallibility. A rational analysis will accept that we
are prone to error and that we need to be able to reflexively criticise our own claims while remaining open to the force of better
arguments. Thus our analyses are objective in the sense that we
take them to be true in so far as we are able to understand them to
be so in the light of evidence, logic and consistency. We are
aspiring for the best possible description and explanation of such

concerns as hunger, starvation and the general absence of needs satisfaction. As such we recognise that our explanations *might* well change in time as better explanations are put forward (Collier, 1994: Chapter 6). Thus part of the task of human security analyses is empirical and part is conceptual. In providing explanations of the causes of these problems we are often dealing with language itself, trying to give an account of why we have come to describe and explain problems in the way that we do. For example, with regard to global communication, neoliberal political economy tells us that we are witnessing an increasingly competitive and open media market that will benefit the consumer and citizen alike (Murdoch, 1994; Collins and Murroni, 1999; Eyre, 1999). Conversely, critics of the neoliberal approach see oligarchic or occasionally monopolistic markets in which powerful corporations are able to control what should be a common or public resource for private power and interests (Melody, 1994; Bagdikian, 1992; Gill, 1995). These contrasting analyses are in part conceptual but they are also in part empirical – simply put, they cannot both be accurate descriptions and explanations of what is taking shape in global communications.[4] Empirical evidence is crucial in allowing us to make rational judgements here. This contrasts with what we can loosely describe as postmodern approaches that would eschew such judgements and argue that we are really dealing with incommensurable discourses that cannot be compared in any meaningful way. The problems with such a view have been addressed by many writers including myself elsewhere and I do not intend to pursue them in depth here (Wilkin, 1999 and 2000). Suffice to say that I find them unpersuasive for a variety of reasons, leaving us with what is ultimately a conservative position, whereby we are able to say anything about anything.[5] If the postmodern analysis is correct then what grounds do I have for accepting their own theoretical position? It is surely only an act of faith as it is not open to rational analysis by way of empirical evidence. Of course empirical issues are necessarily indeterminate as I have already stressed – our knowledge does indeed change over time. But this does not mean that at any given time 'anything goes' by way of explanation. For example, there have been a variety of attempts to explain the causes of the Gulf War that have tended to focus upon the role that various political, economic and cultural factors played. By way of contrast, an explanation that sought to explain the Gulf War by reference to the movement of the stars would have less credibility precisely because it is an argument that provides us with no substantive grounds upon which to evaluate its claims. Empirical study may be indeterminate in the sense that our explanations are always (potentially) open to revision, but this does not mean that we do or should accept all explanations as being equally valid. In practice in our everyday lives we intuitively do not and for good reasons: it is simply implausible.

In attempting to highlight issues of human security we are in part concerned with changing the conceptual framework that we use to understand and explain international relations. It is also about important empirical issues such as, in this instance, the flow of communication, literacy levels, global expenditure on education, patterns of ownership and control of the communications industry, and so on. Thus in epistemological terms we have no grounds for eschewing a rational analysis which attempts to make sense of the key processes and structures that shape global order, raising questions about the adequacy and meaning of the concepts that we use to describe these events. Being rational does not mean the search for an account which is a 'God's eye view of things' (Putnam, 1993 and 1995). On the contrary, any rational analysis will be based upon the concepts and information that we have available to us and from which a number of possible explanations will emerge. This does not mean that there are no grounds for choosing between such understandings and explanations. An explanation of illiteracy or famine that argued that it was simply 'all in the mind' is demonstrably less plausible than one that focuses upon access to, distribution of and control over available resources. Clearly, these are wide debates and I have only offered a sketch here of a theoretical position that might be used to underpin human security studies. In concluding this section it is worth offering a quote that I think addresses the aims and limitations that human security should aspire to:

> At every stage of history our concern must be to dismantle those forms of authority and oppression that survive from an era when they might have been justified in terms of the need for security or survival or economic development, but that now contribute to – rather than alleviate – material and cultural deficit. If so, there will be no doctrine of social change fixed for the present and the future, nor even, necessarily, a specific and unchanging concept of the goals toward which social change would tend. Surely our understanding of the nature of man or of the range of viable social forms is so rudimentary that any far-reaching doctrine must be treated with great scepticism, just as scepticism is in order when we hear that 'human nature' or 'the demands of efficiency' or 'the complexity of modern life' requires this or that form of oppression or autocratic rule. [Chomsky, 1973: 152]

I want to turn now to the theme of communication needs and human security.

## Communication Needs and Human Security

In this section I set out what I take to be central to the concept of communication needs within the context of the possible attainment of human security, before linking this concept to ideas of progress and global communication. Communication needs can best be understood as being structured by three interrelated themes: the means of communication, the quality and quantity of information, and levels of education.

Taking the last theme first, in order for citizens to be able to exercise and extend their democratic freedoms, education is a fundamental prerequisite. Literacy, numeracy and the development of our creative potentials are central to our ability to act as critical, reasoning beings, making judgements about the factors that affect our daily lives. Thus a crucial indicator for human security will be the levels of global expenditure on education and the obstacles to such expenditure. Likewise, in order for citizens to be able to develop their ideas about politics, economy and culture, it is necessary that there is an adequate supply of information that is both diverse and which aims to inform and challenge received opinions. In essence, this is a classic liberal ideal about the need for free speech (Kelley and Donway, 1990). Later in this chapter I turn to an analysis of what is often described as the global flow of information in order to assess the extent to which that flow provides both the quantity and quality of information that citizens need in order to make such judgements. Finally, the means of communication themselves are clearly crucial to the concept of communication needs. The form of ownership and control of the means of communication helps to structure the degree of openness, diversity and accountability of the media to a democratic audience. As I have already analysed, recent developments in global communication have moved the means of communication more firmly than ever into the hands of powerful private institutions, to the detriment of human security. This is a complex issue – the tools of NIT are also increasingly being used by a variety of social and political movements to challenge the entrenched hierarchies that structure the current world order, what Arrighi, Hopkins and Wallerstein (1989) have usefully called anti-systemic movements. There are, then, contradictory tendencies at work here.[6] The key point remains though that it is not enough that people have access to information, they need also to be able to communicate with each other in the wide range of groups and institutions that make up civil society, which is why the ownership and control of the means of communication is so important to human security.

The importance of these three and related themes is that taken together they provide the framework within which citizens can formulate and develop their ideas about politics, economy and culture. This is not to suggest that social change is simply a matter of idealism: the triumph of the best idea. On the contrary, progressive social change such as that mooted by human security is always concerned with the material and the ideational obstacles to human emancipation. No amount of free speech will *directly* end illiteracy, poverty or famine, for example. None the less, if we are to defend the idea that citizens must have the resources needed upon which to make such rational judgements, then these three themes would seem to be pivotal.

It is worth pausing here to clarify what I mean by a rational judgement as again this idea has been under attack in modern social and political thought for some time. The critic might ask if the idea of rational judgement is simply the ability of powerful nations, institutions, groups or discourses to impose their norms upon subordinate or alternate social classes and alternative forms of knowledge (Rorty, 1991). This, or something like it, is a common refrain to which rationalists have had to respond. It seems to me that there are a number of grounds on which a fairly simple and powerful defence of rationality can be made. A rational judgement is one which reflects the following: it is open to criticism; the person holding the view is prepared to listen to criticism, and revise their opinions in the light of better or more powerful explanations and understandings of the matters at hand, and that a person bases their beliefs wherever possible on the available information and forms of knowledge. Being rational in our judgements means no more and no less than recognising our fallibility and the need to find grounds for the beliefs that we hold. As Brian Fay has written:

> All rational inquirers will not necessarily agree with one another. To be rational is to have good reasons for one's beliefs, together with an openness to reconsider alternatives, and a willingness to revise one's beliefs if evidence is adduced which fits better with an alternative system of beliefs. To be rational is to be informed about the relevant facts, clear headed conceptually, impartial, open-minded, consistent, and accountable to the evidence as responsibly as one can; A group of people possessing these characteristics would not necessarily agree with one another; but this does not show that their beliefs are not rationally based, or that they are not rational creatures ... Rational beings can disagree with one another and still be rational as long as they are willing to submit their beliefs to argument and debate, as long as their adherence to their beliefs is consistent with the evidence as they best know it, and as long as they are on the lookout for other beliefs which square better with the evidence. Rational people are those who are uncertain of the truth of their beliefs, and who are open to revising them. [Fay, 1987: 179]

This does not preclude the fact that powerful classes and states can and do attempt to impart a world-view concerning how we should live that largely reflects their own particular elite interests. Rationality and our ability to exercise reason are not absolutes, but are subject to all kinds of pressures and problems. None the less, the fact that we are capable of acting irrationally does not invalidate rationality *per se*. What it does illustrate is that there are both material and ideational obstacles that confront us when we attempt to exercise our rational powers. We are also capable of recognising ideological attempts to legitimise hierarchies of power in society when they confront us.

Thus if human security depends in part upon recognising and defending our communication needs (that is, communication, information and education), it is also inherently tied up with the possibility of progress in human history. What then, do we mean by progress and what role does communication play in its attainment?

As with many strands of Enlightenment social and political thought, it has become fashionable to disparage notions of progress in contemporary social and political theory. Generally, ideas of progress are criticised on one of two grounds: first, that the concept usually reflects the ideas of dominant groups in world order, a form of cultural imperialism; second, progress is disparaged by those who see only cycles of horror and destruction in the course of human history. At the end of a century of unparalleled global conflict it is not hard to understand why such views should be held, but in their own way they are as flawed as those who would see only an uninterrupted onward march of progress in human affairs (Gray, 1999: 166–9). Human security as a concept is by definition concerned with progress and social justice. As the earlier quote from Chomsky illustrates, progress is not teleological, towards some end point in human history beyond which change will not occur. On the contrary, human security posits a notion of progress that is ongoing and transformatory. The task is to construct the kind of institutions, procedures and structures that enable all people to take meaningful part in the decisions that shape our lives. Only on such a basis can anything like solidarity around questions of social justice be established.

Habermas's work on the evolution of morality is informative here for human security and its concern with global communications (Habermas, 1979). Habermas has mapped out in a persuasive work the way in which moral consciousness as a global phenomenon has developed over the centuries. The key point that Habermas is making here is that despite the horrors of human history, there is plenty of evidence to illustrate the ways in which it has been possible for people to learn from history and move beyond practices that are now taken to be unacceptable. Slavery, racism and sexism are all examples of the way in which human societies have struggled to overturn established forms of oppression, however much this is both uneven and ongoing (Habermas, 1999). Slavery, for example, is practised and has been targeted by the International Labour Organisation, among others, for its complete abolition (ILO, 1997). Habermas's point is not that moral progress is inevitable or that material improvements in people's lives are irrelevant to a good society. Rather, he is rendering clear the idea that there are distinct tendencies towards progress in human affairs that can and must be mapped by progressive social movements. Human security must also learn this lesson in its attempt to defend the centrality of human needs and autonomy for the idea of global social justice.

The global communications industries play an unprecedented role in this area and one that is deeply problematic. To the extent that we gain information about world affairs, most evidence suggests that we gain it through the mainstream news media that is itself largely dominated by institutions and actors based in the core capitalist states. Writers such as Roland Robertson and Anthony Giddens have written about the emergence of a global moral consciousness in which ordinary citizens are increasingly able to respond to major global issues, whether environmental disasters or civil wars, bringing pressure to bear on their respective governments to act to bring aid to such problems (Robertson, 1992; Giddens, 1994). The main mediating influence here is the global communications industry and this raises important questions about power and autonomy. If citizens are to act in an autonomous manner when it comes to issues of politics, economy and culture, they need to be able to think and act upon the basis of open, plural and critical information about such affairs. The key question here is: to what extent do developments in global communications help or hinder the possibility of the mainstream news media performing such a role? Clearly this is a potentially vast question but it is central to human security and its concern with human autonomy given the all-embracing role that global communications plays in our lives. I will address this particular issue shortly but I want to conclude this section by turning to the ways in which progress in human security can be evaluated as a concept.

The United Nations' Human Development Report Index (UNHDRI) has become perhaps the most widely quoted source of statistical information on the indices that shape human life. Published annually, it provides us with a wide-ranging and often deeply critical analysis of global human development. However, in terms of human security and its concerns with progress it has a number of significant weaknesses that must be acknowledged. Human security in general is concerned with poverty in all of its forms and this is not something that can be viewed solely in quantitative terms. Poverty is as much about the quality of life as it is simply about the distribution of material goods. The UNHDRI seeks to offer a guide for the measurement of poverty that raises some concern. For example, global poverty is defined in terms of those living on less than US$1 dollar per day (UNDP, 1997).[7] This scale matches that of the World Bank's major study on global poverty, which was due to be followed up in September 2000 (World Bank, 1990). Anyone living on more than this sum is not considered to be living in poverty. Thus it has enabled the authors to argue that global poverty is decreasing (UNDP, 1997: 2–3). As Canadian political economist Michel Chossudovsky has written, this severely distorts our understanding of the depth of global poverty in material terms and in terms of the quality of people's lives (Chossudovsky, 1997: 42–3). In part, this may well be explained by the politically constrained nature of mainstream UN publications such as the *Human Development Report*, though even then it should be acknowledged that the findings of these reports are still vital sources of information on global poverty. It is not the intention of this book to set out a detailed program for the evaluation of poverty but it would seem to me that human security studies must consider the question of poverty and development in the following ways:

- Poverty and uneven development are tendencies integrated by the institutions, structures and procedures that shape all four levels of world order.

- The deepening inequalities of wealth and poverty that have scarred world order in the past two decades are deeply problematic for social justice as they reinforce hierarchies of political and economic power in global social relations. These hierarchies of power systematically empower some at the expense of others, as I will illustrate shortly when I turn to the question of communication needs.

- Poverty eradication should be concerned with the maximisation of human need satisfaction, not simply strategies designed to satisfy basic human needs.

- A causal analysis of poverty is vital to human security and must focus its concern upon the major mechanisms that underpin global poverty (UNDP, 1997). In the area of communication, it seems reasonably clear that there are two primary mechanisms that are central to challenging communication poverty – the geopolitical structure of the inter-state system and the property relations that are at the heart of global capitalism. In systemic terms, states tend primarily to be guided by some conception of the national interest, and corporations by the drive for profit.

Neither are primarily concerned with *general* human need satisfaction and both present us with major institutional, structural
and procedural obstacles to it. I will illustrate these claims in the
remainder of this chapter but there is plenty of detailed and
critical analysis in other areas of global development (health,
housing, and welfare) that would suggest that these two major
causal mechanisms are at the heart of existing global poverty.

Having set out these issues, it is important to consider the idea of
global communications and what they potentially offer human
security. If the goal of human security is to be a viable one, then
what, given existing resources and capacities, should we optimally
expect from global communications and to what extent does it
meet those expectations?

Given the undoubted breakthroughs in communications offered
us by NIT, it is reasonable to speculate that the potential is there to
support the goals of human security. Global communication could
service the ideal of providing us with an open, plural, critical and
independent form of news media and channels of communication
that could help to sustain and inform a critical global citizenry.
Indeed, much of the contemporary writing upon global civil society
depends exactly upon this possibility being or becoming real. The
mechanisms that now exist through NIT provide us with the means
for a complex and cosmopolitan global dialogue between peoples in
which issues of development and social justice could be discussed
and acted upon in a historically unprecedented fashion.

Human security depends upon obtaining just social relations as
a means to remove or mitigate many of the fundamental causes of
social conflict. In order to obtain such relations, solidarity between
peoples at the four levels of world order is of paramount importance. Abstracting peoples into discrete nations has historically
served to divide them in the face of what are often common
problems. In fomenting a debate on these issues, human security
does not seek to foreclose the range of options that such a dialogue
might consider with regard to the form that just social relations
might take. As Charles Tilly has written in an important work on
the rise of the European state system, there are reasons and
evidence to suggest that the modern nation-state might well be in
a period of transformation into new forms of social organisation
(Tilly, 1997: Chapter 1). If this is so, then it is crucial for the possibility of progress and human security that such debates are open to
diverse ideas and discussions. However, the evidence at hand is not
supportive of this possibility and the remainder of the chapter will
focus on the problems that global communications present for the
possibility of human security in general and human autonomy in
particular.

## Developments in the Political Economy of Education

Given what I have set out thus far in my concern with the role that autonomy plays in human security, the importance of education and the resources devoted to it cannot be underestimated. Debates about the form of education and how it should be organised are too complex to enter into here so it will be sufficient to focus upon the key developments in the political economy of education as they have occurred in recent decades. For human security and its concern with human progress, it is hard to get away from the view that education should ultimately be about three major principles:

- Providing people with the necessary skills and competencies that they need in order to make sense of and question their world;
- Providing them with the means by which they can enter into the diverse aspects of their society, and
- Enabling people to exercise their various creative talents and skills to the fullest possible use.

The political economy of education raises a number of important questions here including: How is educational service to be provided? How do we allocate resources to education in relation to other important areas such as health and welfare? Who controls and determines the content of education? While the aspiration towards attaining basic levels of global literacy is a crucial step along the way, it is important not to lose sight of the fact that this is only a stepping stone on the way to expanding educational provision for all. What then have been the key trends in global educational expenditure over the past two decades? Further, what is meant by the idea of communication poverty?

The most in-depth analysis of these problems is the ongoing programme established by the World Education Forum, a global mechanism established under the auspices of UNESCO, to set the goals of universal educational standards. Set up in 1990, this programme has sought to promote common goals around the elimination of illiteracy, eradicating the gender imbalance over access to education, ensuring that children receive the primary and secondary education that they need, and so on. Its first meeting was held at Jomtien in Thailand in March 1990, and it drew representatives of the global educational community. In April 2000, a decade review of progress made towards these goals was held at Dakar in Senegal and the conclusions with regard to progress on raising educational standards was decidedly mixed (UNESCO, 2000). There are various methodological problems with evaluating the success and failure of the project, as 'success' was frequently defined in the terms of particular countries rather than by establishing a universal standard. As

the report argues, '"success" in these circumstances, requires interpretation from many different standpoints as well as complex
judgements about a large and varied body of data' (UNESCO, 2000:
11). None the less, the representatives at the initial Jomtien meeting
were able to agree upon six universal targets for education:

- Expansion of early childhood care and developmental abilities,
  including family and community interventions, especially for
  poor, disadvantaged and disabled children;
- Universal access to, and completion of, primary (or whatever
  higher level of education is considered as 'basic') by the year 2000;
- Improvement of learning achievement such that an agreed
  percentage of an age cohort (for example, 80 per cent of 14-year-
  olds) attains or surpasses a defined level of necessary learning
  achievement;
- Reduction of the adult illiteracy rate (the appropriate age-group
  to be determined in each country) to, say, one-half of its 1990
  level by the year 2000, with sufficient emphasis on female
  literacy to significantly reduce the current disparity between
  male and female illiteracy rates;
- Expansion of provision of basic education and training in other
  essential skills required by youths and adults, with programme
  effectiveness assessed in terms of behavioural change and impact
  on health, employment and productivity, and
- Increased acquisition by individuals and families of the knowledge, skills and values required for better living and sound and
  sustainable development, made available through all education
  channels including the mass media, other forms of modern and
  traditional communication, and social action, with effectiveness
  assessed in terms of behavioural change. (UNESCO, 2000: 13)

Taking each point in turn, the *World Educational Report 2000* notes
that progress has been mixed in accord with both cultural factors of
distinct states and societies, and also in terms of the wider political-
economic framework within which public educational institutions
have to act. For example, with regard to the first of the universal
principles the report concludes that

> ... inevitably much of the concern that has been expressed in the
> reports of progress since Jomtien relates to the difficulties many
> countries or parts of countries are experiencing. Making
> adequate provision for access and participation by learners and
> for teachers to be adequately prepared, equipped and resourced
> to carry out their work is still a monumental challenge in many
> countries and areas. These difficulties reflect conditions and
> circumstances which in part are beyond the educational system
> itself. [UNESCO, 2000: 17]

Time after time the report concludes that with regard to the six key provisions, progress is uneven and often small, with significant areas of the world going backwards in terms of educational indicators, most notably Sub-Saharan Africa and the Eastern European countries. The problem of inequality of educational opportunity and provision not only remains but as the report somewhat ruefully observes, 'closer analysis of the data reveals continuing, sometimes increasing, inequitable provision and practice. Indeed, the problem has grown' (UNESCO, 2000: 55).

In 1997, global illiteracy stood at 850 million people, with over 100 million in industrial societies. As an overall percentage of the world's population, there has been an encouraging shift towards increasing levels of literacy with the total figure for global adult literacy increasing from 64 per cent in 1990 to 76 per cent in 1997 (UNDP, 1999: 22). In turn, this raises important causal questions about the major obstacles to attaining such goals. It is beyond the ambitions of this book to offer an extended treatise on comparative global educational standards. Comparative analysis of educational standards remains a highly contentious and politicised debate with examples of comparatively poor countries achieving significantly higher standards of educational competence than comparatively wealthy countries. For example, in the mid-1980s the Sandinista government in Nicaragua introduced a relatively low-cost and wide-ranging nationwide literacy campaign that was highly successful in terms of its goals and which received major awards and acclaim from international education and charitable bodies for its progress in eradicating illiteracy. It was ultimately undermined by the US-sponsored proxy war on Nicaragua carried out under the Reagan presidencies which forced the Nicaraguan government to concentrate ever more resources on defence and to abandon its popular and populist social and education programmes (Melrose, 1985). The cost of providing global educational access is far from being exorbitant as the *Human Development Report* has illustrated in a powerful way on numerous occasions. The key question that remains to be addressed then is: *what are the major causal mechanisms prohibiting the attainment of the goals of the World Educational Forum?*

The *Human Development Report* concedes that while public services in general have been under severe pressure globally it remains crucial that states are committed to investment in education. As the report concedes, 'in OECD countries the problem is that globalisation has pulled back on state services and pushed more to private services. Many social commentators protest the ensuing deterioration in quality' (UNDP, 2000: 79). The 'enabling' state has as a primary task for neoliberals the role of providing citizens with the skills necessary to make themselves saleable as workers in the global labour marketplace. Interestingly, despite the

*Human Development Repport's* concerns about the need for investment in education to eradicate global illiteracy, when seen in
comparative terms, the costs appear to be minuscule. The *Report*
itself illustrated this in stark fashion in Table 3.1, on comparative
global expenditure in 1998 (UNDP, 1998: 37).

**Table 3.1  Comparative annual global expenditure in US$ billions**

| | |
|---|---|
| Basic education for all | 6 |
| Cosmetics in the US | 8 |
| Water and sanitation for all | 9 |
| Ice cream in Europe | 11 |
| Reproductive health for all women | 12 |
| Perfumes in Europe and the US | 12 |
| Basic health and nutrition | 13 |
| Pet foods in the US and Europe | 17 |
| Business entertainment in Japan | 35 |
| Cigarettes in Europe | 50 |
| Alcoholic drinks in Europe | 105 |
| Narcotic drugs in the world | 400 |
| Military spending in the world | 780 |

*Source*: UNDP, 1998: 37.

These figures appear to be quite striking at first, particularly in an
era when the neoliberal political economic orthodoxy imposes a
systemic strait-jacket around governments, which seeks to impose
limits to public expenditure on such areas as education, health and
welfare (Gray, 1998; Scholte, 2000: 26–9). To this end, *The
Economist* has recently noted how developments in NIT enable both
companies and individuals to avoid paying taxes, a trend which the
magazine sees as likely to increase in the years ahead (*Economist*,
2000c). At the same time, however, it appears that there are sufficient public resources to spend US$ 780 billion per annum on
global military expenditure (Thomas, 1999: 244). This is a shocking
sum, that in itself raises the obvious question that if this figure is
meant to bring global security why is it that the world has been and
continues to be riven with continuous conflicts? The retort from
defenders of this military expenditure would no doubt be to claim
that things would be much worse without this sum being spent.
What it fails to present us with is a plausible explanation as to the
causes of war and social conflict. In practice, military expenditure
amounts to dealing with the effects of social conflict or an attempt
at containing the global social inequalities that help generate
conflict. The argument provided by proponents of global military
expenditure is that conflict is either inherent to human beings, a
product of our natures, or is the result of the anarchic nature of the
international system where no single authority governs and

enforces the rule of law. Both of these arguments are inadequate for distinct reasons: first, our understanding of human nature is limited and definitive statements on this question remain problematic; second, the international system has been clearly structured by geopolitics (inter-state competition) and the anarchy of capitalist production which leads to the social inequalities and hierarchies that increasingly structure world order.

Looking at the geopolitical issue, world order has been structured through the power and authority of the world's core capitalist states and continues to be so. World order is a product of this power structure, largely shaped by the core Western states under the leadership of the United States. Questions of international law and justice at the international institutional level have tended to flow from this arrangement. Hence, the ongoing NATO involvement in Yugoslavia is seen as legitimate because it has been defined as being so largely by the United States and the United Kingdom through the mechanism of NATO. This is not to argue that international law and justice are irrelevant or that we can simply conclude that all such rules are mere reflections of the interests of powerful states. On the contrary, questions of international law and justice are crucial to the possibility of human security being attained. What this does illustrate is that when it comes to key issues in world order and the overarching interests of the core capitalist states and their corporations, then international law and justice have historically tended to be ignored or sidelined (Evans, 1998).

We can see then that world order is structured by two interlocking systems: the geopolitical structure of the inter-state system and the system of capitalist production. As should be clear this is a question of political economy in which global social relations are defined by their relationship to the major political and economic institutions and procedures – systems that are never simply static. Developments are always taking place within the systems that help produce, reproduce and transform the ways in which global social relations take place. Failure to recognise the fact that these are procedures with an unfolding history and movement can lead to the kind of reified analysis that is common in international relations theory (Griffiths, 1992). It is hardly surprising, given such simplistic views, that the fall of the Soviet Union was viewed as being such a major blow to orthodox realist accounts of international relations. States never willingly surrender power, we are told, they are perennial power maximisers! An approach to international relations which is not sensitive to the unfolding nature of complex global social relations as realised through the interaction of states, capitalist markets and social groups can hardly offer an adequate explanation of such events, given that it is locked into a view of history in which states appear as largely unchanging and irreducible entities.

If there are, then, massive resources available to satisfy human needs such as education and literacy, as these figures clearly suggest, then the question remains as to why more is not being done to bring this about? What are the causal mechanisms blocking this possibility? In counter-factual terms, there is strong evidence to support the argument that we could satisfy human needs for education and by extension, autonomy, so why don't we? In order to answer this question, we must focus our attention upon the actors, ideologies and institutions that control these resources and this leads us to a reasonably clear answer: the structures, procedures, institutions and actors that dominate and structure global economic production and geopolitical policy are the primary mechanisms for shaping global social relations. Taking these two processes (global capitalism and the inter-state system) as part of the total structure of a historically evolving world order, we must focus our attention upon the principles that underpin these processes. Turning to global production first, an important contradiction exists between global capitalism and human security. Global capitalism is driven by the need of firms to acquire profit, not by the desire to satisfy human needs. The latter is a contingent outcome of global capitalist relations, hence its uneven nature in practice. A dominant tendency in global capitalist relations has been towards overproduction and underconsumption. As companies have sought higher profits and capital accumulation, this has come about through expanding their market power and reach and also through an assault upon the wealth of working and non-working people. Thus, in the early 1990s, we witnessed a period of global recession and mass unemployment while at the same time the world's major corporations, overwhelmingly based in the core capitalist states, were enjoying record profits. Capital could be accumulated by sacking people or replacing them with NIT and cutting the wages bill. In the short term, this can succeed, but in the long term the obvious contradiction here is that it reduces the general demand for goods and services. When new jobs have been created, it is far from clear that they will be at comparable wage levels. There comes a point at which this contradiction raises major social conflict and political turmoil. When we turn to the realm of global public policy we find that the public institutions that are in theory there to protect the public have historically been battlegrounds within which conflicting social groups have sought to direct public policy towards sharply contrasting ends. Polanyi famously called this the 'double-movement', in which subordinate social groups have sought to tame capitalist markets because of their socially destructive consequences. In order to understand what drives public policy, we must abandon a concern with the abstractions of rational choice policy formation and recognise that such decisions are taken within the context of existing social relations: they are structured by existing forms of social power. As Wallerstein acutely observed, the history of the world can be seen as being one of a series of struggles against inequality, something that structures both the geopolitical system and global capitalist production (Wallerstein, 1979: 49). These entrenched hierarchies of social power are embedded in the structures, institutions and procedures that govern all four levels of world order. *If human security is to be a viable goal, then a transformation of these structures, institutions and procedures would appear to be a necessary requirement.* As the World Educational Forum concedes, any project with the ambition of attaining universal education standards must be sensitive to the differences of culture and belief that help to structure the world's social relations (UNESCO, 2000: 18). However, without addressing the problems caused by the contradictions inherent in the inter-state system and the tendency of global capitalism to polarise social relations and prioritise private power over public need, it seems unlikely that the necessary material resources needed for such a project will ever be made available. As I will illustrate in the final chapter, the seeds of possibility for such a transformation are already a part of world order and, however weak they may appear when compared to the powerful states and companies that structure existing global social relations, these movements are significant.

I want to turn now to the political economy of communication itself. This is a crucial issue for reasons set out by Leo Bogart who argued that 'the ideas and images that the mass media disseminate shape collective life, form social values and determine the course of history' (Bogart, 1994: 16).

## Global Communication, Information and Human Security

The major question here for human security and global communication is the extent to which prevailing trends are leading towards the satisfaction of communication needs. For neoliberal political economy, the extension of capitalist market mechanisms into wider areas of communication is a necessary factor in the increased competition, efficiency, diversity and openness of media forms globally; hence the emphasis in recent successive Rounds of the General Agreement on Tariffs and Trade (GATT) and the subsequent World Trade Organization (WTO) upon the liberalisation, privatisation and deregulation of the communications markets (Herman and McChesney, 1997: 50–52, 112–14). Equally, the extension of private-sector initiatives into education has become a theme that connects a number of developed and developing countries alike. Critics of the neoliberal political economy world-view are diverse, of course, and so cannot be easily grouped under a single heading, though writers such as Vincent Mosco have tended to use the over-worked term of 'critical political economy' to group them (Mosco, 1996). As should be clear by now, it is evident that for human security the neoliberal political-economy model offers neither an accurate description of prevailing trends in global communication nor a prescriptive vision of the good society that allows for the idea that a good society is one in which all people can be seen as winners. For the neoliberal world-view, life is ultimately a competition in which the rewards go to the winners in what is (ideally) a race in which all can compete on an equal basis. For human security, there are two fundamental flaws in this neoliberal vision, one descriptive and the other prescriptive.

## Neoliberal Political Economy – Idealised Brutality

Taking the neoliberal vision's descriptive weakness first, when we turn to capitalist markets in general and communication markets in particular the neoliberal faith in competition is severely under-mined. William Lazonick talks of capitalist markets as guided markets in which production, distribution and investment are structured through the actions of the dominant corporations in that particular market (Lazonick, 1991). Rather than a never-ending competition in which innovation and efficiency are promoted by independent entrepreneurs, what we find instead are markets in which there is competition between large-scale corporations, over-whelmingly based in the core capitalist states, taking the form of an oligarchy in which the powerful few set the rules and standards for the subordinate many. The communications industries are classic examples of this, as we have already noted. In telecommunications, for example, as we saw in Chapter 2, the ongoing mergers and concentration of ownership and control of the global telecommu-nications corporations leaves us with a market dominated by companies from the core capitalist states.

Likewise, if we turn to the media entertainment markets, we find that a handful of companies tend to dominate production, distri-bution and investment and that in structural terms these are trends that have been exacerbated in the past twenty years (McChesney, 1999). For example, taking the cinema industry in the mid-1970s, there was far more competition between Europe, Japan, India and the US in global terms than there is today. How, then, did these changes come about? In neoliberal terms, the US cinema industry succeeds simply because it gives people what they want at the most efficient means. In reality, this is a naive view of global political economy that leaves the question of social power out of its analysis. The dominance of the US cinema industry has come about through the conscious activities of the Hollywood system seeking to exert political influence over successive US administrations to use their global power to influence international trade legislation so as to suit the interests and power of American cinema. In practical terms, this has led to the dominance of US cinema and the marginalisation of its main competitors. This does not mean that there are not sizeable alternatives to Hollywood's dominance of cinema markets. There are significant cinema and television corporations in Brazil, India and China, for example. However, the US cinema is the only truly global actor, with the power to set standards for trade and investment and also to establish global patterns for the consumption of cultural goods.

What we can see from this example is the thinness and idealised nature of the neoliberal political economy as a description of how global markets work. In practice, capitalist markets are dominated by the world's most powerful corporations. Again, Table 3.2 is illustrative here.

**Table 3.2 Global distribution of the world's ultra-rich, 1997**

| Region or country group | Distribution of 225 richest people | Combined wealth of ultra-rich ($US billion) | Average wealth of ultra-rich ($US billion) |
|---|---|---|---|
| OECD | 143 | 637 | 4.5 |
| Asia | 43 | 233 | 5.4 |
| Latin America and the Caribbean | 22 | 55 | 2.5 |
| Arab states | 11 | 78 | 7.1 |
| Eastern Europe and the CIS | 4 | 8 | 2.0 |
| Sub-Saharan Africa | 2 | 4 | 2.0 |
| Total | 225 | 1015 | 23.5 |

*Source*: UNDP, 1998: 30

In the communications markets, the same general tendency illustrated in Table 3.2 holds true: the markets are overwhelmingly dominated by corporations based in the core capitalist states. While these general tendencies hold true, even some critics of capitalist markets would concede that in terms of innovation, risk and the proliferation of commodities, capitalist markets are more efficient mechanisms and more responsive to consumer demands than alternate forms of production based on cooperation or mutual aid might be. However, if we look more closely at the proliferation of commodities in the communications markets, even this claim is far from straightforward. Many of the most significant innovations in communications in the past century have actually emerged in the public sector and through publicly funded research, only to be subsequently taken up by private companies. Such developments as satellites and FM radio were the result of publicly funded research; even the Internet itself, now seen by many companies as the most significant factor fuelling the next industrial revolution, as it has recently been described in *The Economist*, was the result of military research (*Economist*, 2000d). There is, then, no *inherent* reason why capitalist markets and private companies should be more innovative or efficient than socially owned or publicly funded institutions.

If, then, the neoliberal description of how capitalist markets function is inaccurate, how do they work in practice? When we examine the structure of global communications markets, what we see emerging is a picture of ownership, control and policy formation that reflects what we can call a form of corporate mercantile capitalism. A clear and mutually reinforcing relationship exists between the interests of the world's major political and corporate agents that results in a coalition of political-economic forces that structure the rules and regulations that shape the world's capitalist markets. Unsurprisingly, these rules and regulations are not intended to promote a general competition in which these already powerful core states and corporations might conceivably 'lose out' to lesser rivals. On the contrary, the rules and regulations are specific: they are intended to allow for the continued dominance and control of markets by the already powerful corporate actors that are largely based in the core G7 states. In practice, the last thing that these core capitalist states and corporations want is a competition that they might lose. Thus we are presented with a far more sophisticated form of corporate mercantile capitalist world order in which the core capitalist states and their major corporations organise production and investment through an elaborate system of negotiated rules and regulations. This is not to suggest that such a system is either all-powerful or permanent in structure. For example, William H. Melody describes the global communications market as an 'indeterminate, unstable oligopoly' (Melody, 1994), that is a market in which a number of extremely powerful communications corporations compete with each other in order to dominate global markets but do so in such a way that they might potentially risk their own financial survival. For example, the recent AOL-Time-Warner merger took place between two heavily indebted companies. Time-Warner held debts at the time of US$17.8 billion while AOL had a comparatively mild US$341 million, prompting one analyst in *Forbes* magazine to ask, 'doesn't anyone care about the debt load anymore?' (Granfield, 2000; Solomon, 2000). In addition to this, media markets in the past 15 years have been subject to repeated takeovers and mergers that have often proven to have unsettling effects on share prices, among other things. Neoliberal ideology would have us believe that corpo-

rations and governments are at best uneasy allies and often practically enemies, with the latter taxing and undermining the
efficiency and innovation of the former. Remember the quote from
Jacques Maison Rouge that pointed out that existing political structures are behind the changes in the global economy and inhibit the
maximisation of corporate efficacy. What Maison Rouge and other
neoliberals actually mean is that the problem with governments is
that they can still be responsive to wider social demands and set
standards for employment, health and safety, working hours and so
on, in order to prevent workers from being openly exploited by
their employers. Clearly this degree of democratic leverage over
public policy by working people inhibits a corporation's power to
pursue profits and is therefore in conflict with its primary goals.
None the less we find that in reality, corporations are invariably
highly dependent upon their national governments to supply them
with a number of provisions:

- The protection and promotion of their interests in international
  trade fora such as GATT and WTO. For example, the corporate
  sponsorship of the recent WTO summit at Seattle is a good indi-
  cation of the normalising of corporate influence over public
  policy.[8]
- The promotion of social order in the domestic sphere by both
  coercion and consent and help to legitimise changes to work
  practices, employment patterns and so on. Britain in the 1980s
  under successive Thatcher administrations is a good example of
  this kind of governance and social restructuring (Gilmour, 1992).
- The provision of an educated workforce possessed of a range of
  competencies necessary in order to allow a capitalist economy to
  function ('the enabling state').

This governmental role is one which connects a new form of
common sense in the most powerful international economic fora
and is similar to the picture set out by former US Trade Secretary
Robert Reich at the beginning of the Clinton presidency (Reich,
1992). In what was seen as a 'Third Way' between a form of brutal
capitalism and overly restrictive state intervention, the role of
governments in the 'new economy' would be that of an enabling
one (Gilbert and Gilbert, 1989). Governments would provide their
citizens with the necessary skills and competencies that they needed
in order to 'enable' them to become attractive to potential employers
(Giddens, 1999). What such a picture of political economy presents
us with is an attempt to legitimise the view that workers have no
right to control the terms of their employment or to have decisions
over conditions of pay, forms of investment, what is to be produced,
and so on. In technical terms, it presents us with the idea of capitalism as a successful machine in which workers must adapt

themselves as cogs where needed in order to make the production process work in return for an income. The question arises here as to whose interests such a system represents. The answer, I would suggest, is that it primarily represents and defends the interests of those who have the power to construct the rules and regulations that determine production and trade in a global economy.

Corporate mercantile capitalism is not simply an extension of older forms of mercantilism that saw nation-states pitched into military and trade conflict with each other (Holton, 1992). There seems little likelihood of Japan, the US and Europe entering into military conflict with each other in the twenty-first century. On the contrary, what we have is a form of global economy in which there have been important *qualitative transformations* in the course of the twentieth century. The most important of these developments was the emergence of a transnational political and economic class that connects the main regions of political, economic and cultural power. Only China and the former Soviet Union were historically excluded from these trends in the twentieth century and although they were an important exception in the past there are clear signs that both of these nation-states will be brought on board in the twenty-first century. As international organisations proliferated in the course of the twentieth century and as writers such as Robert Cox (1987), Stephen Gill (1990) and Craig Murphy (1994) recognised, they tended to promote a more transnational approach to issues of political economy. A variety of public and private international organisations enabled the emergence and promotion of a more transnational class outlook among sections of the governing classes and political elites in world order and are now at the heart of current debates of what is often termed 'global governance' (Pagden, 1998; Hewson and Sinclaire, 1999; Thomas, 2000). Global governance is said to refer to the range of rules, regulations and norms that underpin world order and the behaviour of governments and peoples within it. Global governance suggests an idea beyond that of simply national government and refers to both the formal and informal mechanisms that structure world order. In practical terms, global governance is neoliberal global governance, the attempt since the collapse of the Bretton Woods system in 1971 by a significant bloc of political and economic elites in the core capitalist states to normalise a new common sense for the organisation of world order which reflects the neoliberal ideology set out in Chapter 2 (Gill, 1995; Chomsky, 1994). Again it needs to be emphasised that it is developments in the means of communication that have enabled this powerful global civil society of elite actors and their institutions to develop as they have done.

These trends do not mean that there is not antagonism between the elites of the core capitalist states and their corporations. On the contrary, what it does allow for is the means by which these core capitalist states and their corporations can resolve their conflicts short of open warfare. Many major trade disputes have arisen between the US, Japan and Europe in the past decade over such goods as foodstuffs, car production and communications commodities (*Business Week*, 1998a). These international institutions allow for these disputes to be settled by the exercise of political and economic power rather than military, to use Mann's (1986) typology. Pressure exerted by the representatives of the core capitalist state powers at the closing of the last GATT Round is a good example of the ways in which political, ideological and economic power can be used to coerce, persuade or compel weaker states to submit to the rules and regulations put forward by the core capitalist states, largely under US leadership. Examples include the conflicts between France and the US over cultural goods, notably cinema and television; and also the conflicts between Europe, the US and the peripheral states over agricultural subsidies. As a consequence, what emerges is a structure of world trade in which the core capitalist states and their corporations are able to construct the rules and regulations of global production, trade, investment and taxation to suit the interests of their dominant social groups. When I use the term 'interests' here it is a necessary reification. If we do not talk about interests in this way, it becomes almost impossible to say anything in our analyses of social, political and economic life. It does not mean that interests cannot be contradictory or that they do not change over time, but it does recognise that social groups can share interests in common for strategic and structural reasons.[9] More specifically here we need to recognise that the interests of national governments and their major corporations are not necessarily synonymous with the interests of their populations as a whole. The interests of companies under capitalism are private: to make a profit and to dominate markets and any competition that might emerge there, not primarily to produce goods and services in order to satisfy people's needs or to encourage global human security. The latter is at best a contingent outcome of global capitalism, not a necessary one. In practice, it is difficult to see how it could be brought about without dramatic transformations in the principles that underpin global capitalism and the inter-state system. Before turning to the prescriptive weakness of neoliberal political economy and its analysis of global communication, I want to give an outline of the key trends in patterns of ownership, control and the flow of global communication.

Since the Second World War there has been a major tension at the heart of international, now global, communications policy. International communications policy can be seen as lasting until the mid-1970s and being largely concerned with the regulation of flows of information between nation-states, while from the mid-1970s onwards global communication has increasingly come to the fore, largely driven by the interests of what have become global communications corporations. The tension that has existed reflects the inequalities of power that have shaped world order in this period, largely, but not exclusively, between the core capitalist states and their companies and the rest of the world. The latter can be viewed in various forms as the Third World, South, Socialist Bloc, and so on: each of these descriptions has its strengths and weaknesses (Wallerstein, 1974). Communication policy has been shaped by two interlocking factors in this period: geopolitics and political economy. In geopolitical terms, the Western bloc of core states under US leadership defended a principle of the free flow of information as the basis for international communications policy. This can be seen as a defence of the classic liberal idea of free speech: under a free flow of information, no single institution or centre of power would be able to control what people came to see, think, hear or believe. From such a basis it was assumed that progress, in general, would emerge. Thus, the United States and the other core capitalist states largely supported UNESCO and free flow as the means to enable people to defend and satisfy their rights to communication as laid down in the new UN Charters of Human Rights. Crucially, Article 19 of the UN Charter enshrines the right to the following:

- Defence of free expression,
- Freedom to hold opinion,
- Freedom to gather information,
- Freedom to receive information,
- The right to impart information and ideas. (Hamelink, 1994a: Chapter 11)

However, for the bloc of semi-peripheral and peripheral capitalist and socialist states, the idea of a free flow of information had very little to do with guaranteeing people's right to communication and everything to do with promoting and defending the right of the communications corporations of the core capitalist states to dominate international and then global markets. Given the hierarchically structured nature of communications markets and the enormous power of those companies already dominant within them, there could be no competition between communications companies on anything like an international scale. The flow of information would be seriously unbalanced and largely dominated by the actions and interests of the corporations of core capitalist states. In response to this, a loose coalition of states and non-governmental organisations (NGOs) formed in the early 1970s and began to formulate policy ideas promoting a *balanced* flow of information to ensure that there was a communication *dialogue* between

the North and South rather than the existing *monologue*. These
plans took the form of what became known as the New World
Information and Communication Order (NWICO) (Alleyne, 1995:
Chapter 6). Given that these ideas were put forward during what is
often described as the period of the Second Cold War, it is perhaps
unsurprising that they were distorted and lambasted in equal
measure first by the US and then the British governments as being
effectively the first step on a path to totalitarian control of the
means of communication, with states controlling journalists and
information alike (Preston et al., 1989). However, the 1999 *Human
Development Report*, which focused its concern on the impact of
globalisation and new technology, noted that whilst in general
there has been an uneven global increase in the use of the means
of communication, inequality of use has increased too. The gap
between both the North and South, or more accurately, the core
capitalist states and the periphery, as well as the gap between the
world's rich and poor, has increased in terms of access to and use of
the means of communication (UNDP, 1999). This finding is
supported by other reports which have noted that the impact of
NIT and the 'new economy' are likely to significantly increase the
wealth and opportunity gap between the world's rich and poor
(Keegan, 1996; BBC News, 1999b; Denny, 2000). The subsequent
developments in the late 1980s and 1990s in communication
inequality confirmed many of the fears of this bloc of NWICO
critics regarding the likely consequences of a free-flow global policy
in communication. Ominously, free flow is now firmly embedded
as the organising principle in the WTO with regard to developments in, for example, telecommunications markets, an area where
we have seen already that an oligopoly of companies from the core
capitalist states dominates (WTO, 1997).

Equally when one looks at the major news agencies that shape
the agenda of what is considered global news on a daily basis we
find that they are based in the core capitalist states: Associated Press
(AP) and United Press International (UPI) are based in the United
States, while Reuters is based in Britain, and Agence-France Presse
(AFP) in France (Boyd-Barrett and Tantanen, 1998). Likewise, in the
fields of entertainment communications corporations we find a
similar pattern of core capitalist state corporations dominating the
production, distribution and exchange of cultural goods and
services (Herman and McChesney, 1997).

Although Time-Warner are often seen as being the largest of
these corporations, precise statistics of the resources and wealth
available to these corporations are notoriously difficult to calculate
as they are all capable of hiding resources around their global
empires in order to avoid paying taxes in their home-base nation-
state. News Corporation, for example, should have paid a global tax

bill in 1998 of Australian $702 million on its $1.95 billion operating profits. Through a variety of inventive accounting schemes
they paid only Australian $260 million (Buckingham, 1999).

These figures indicate a tendency within the free flow of information which confirms the worst fears of its critics. This is a system
within which the means and flow of communication is largely
dictated by the interests of the G7-based communication corporations working wherever possible with their respective state
managers to construct international policy to preserve their social
power. This is an example of the tyranny of the minority.
Communication and information inequality is a structural
outcome of these relations. This does not mean that the interests of
either state managers or corporate actors can simply be reduced to
each other. Clearly it is possible for them to clash, and in the realm
of global communication the ongoing dispute between the US
government and various US-based communications corporations
with Microsoft is a classic example of such an intra-elite conflict.

None the less, the defender of the neoliberal view might well
retort that ultimately none of this really matters. If companies are
giving people what they want then why should we be concerned
with questions of ownership and control of the means of communication? If we are interested in human security then we should be
encouraged by the fact that more forms of communication and
choices are available to people than ever before, enhancing their
ability to make rational, critical and autonomous judgements about
the issues that shape their daily lives. In effect, the current Blair
government in Britain has tended towards taking this position on
the question of ownership and control of the means of communication (Collins and Murroni, 1996; Ramsay, 1998). Such· an
approach makes sense only if we ignore a host of questions about
power, influence and autonomy that one would have thought were
central to theories about democracy. However, the neoliberal claim
has a powerful rhetorical appeal and in order to explain why it is
flawed, we can turn to the conclusions to this chapter and the
weakness of the prescriptive claims that underpin the neoliberal
vision of the good society.

## Conclusions: Obstacles to Human Security – The Limits of the Neoliberal Analysis

As we have seen thus far there is an undoubted tendency among
the mainstream global communication corporations towards an
ever-greater concentration of resources. This is usually described in
the business press as 'synergy', as we saw in Chapter 2. The neoliberal vision of the good society, that is said to spring from the
extension of capitalist markets into wider areas of our lives, reflects

the classic liberal ideal that individuals and their personal liberty are the foundations of any just social order (Nozick, 1974). As such, individual liberty is the primary good underpinning any just society. Further, this defence of individual liberty cannot be sacrificed for any other good such as equality without doing serious harm to individual freedom. The parameters of this debate have been set out in two famous works by John Rawls and Robert Nozick (Rawls, 1973; Nozick, 1974). For the classic liberal, individual liberty enables us as individuals to make rational choices about all areas of life from our beliefs about politics and morality through to the goods that we choose to purchase and consume. If no one is visibly and overtly interfering with my choices then they must be free ones. Furthermore, as a rational individual I am clearly in the best position to decide as to what is in my best interest. In order to maximise my choices, the capitalist market is historically the best mechanism for doing this as it opens up as wide a range of goods and services to me as is possible. If something is wanted by people then there is an incentive for someone to deliver it in return for a profit. The market is the most efficient and responsive mechanism for satisfying people's want and desires and as such is synonymous, in neoliberal thought, with freedom (Friedman, 1962). If this is so then it would seem that capitalist markets are the best mechanism for promoting general human security too, as they are, in neoliberal terms, competitive, efficient, responsive, open and flexible.

As much as Marxist social theory has often been criticised for an overwhelming capitalist logic that drives its analyses of global political economy, so too can the point be made about neoliberal political economy. For neoliberals, capitalism is simply the self-evident choice for rational egoists who are driven by their desire to satisfy their material wants while at the same time preserving their liberty through an institutional infrastructure that places the right to own property at its heart. Even writers such as Francis Fukuyama, who has posited the end of history and the eventual triumph of liberal capitalist democracy on a global scale, see this as an almost inevitable historical outcome (Fukuyama, 1992). This neoliberal story reads as follows: in human history, capitalism has been the most productive system and has ensured the greatest degree of individual liberty for the most people. It is the desire for freedom that drives people in history and capitalism has proven itself to be the system best suited to satisfying this goal both materially and in terms of individual liberty. Capitalist democracy brings us what we really want: peace, prosperity and freedom. Rhetorically, this is undoubtedly a very powerful argument and when we consider it in the light of the expanded role of global communication in all areas of our lives then it becomes even more so. Developments in global communication (potentially) enhance our choices and our ability to coordinate activities in all areas of our lives with those separated by time and space over vast distances. Individual liberty is (potentially) extended at the expense of both the state and corporations as citizens and consumers alike are able to exercise their critical, rational capacities to evaluate political and economic issues. The organisation of the protests against the WTO summit in Seattle 1999 were crucially dependent upon the Internet, for example (Wilkin, 2000).

Given that human security emphasises the role that global social relations and democratic institutions play in our lives and that the only democratic and just arrangements are ideally those agreed upon through consensus and open discussion, the neoliberal vision would seem to provide a definitive answer to the aspirations of human security. So much so that the political-economy question that we began with concerning questions of ownership and control of the means of communications seems to pale into insignificance. Why should we care who owns and controls the means of communication when there is so much variety on offer anyway? Individuals are free to pick and choose as they wish and everything that is wanted or desired can be found in a capitalist marketplace. Autonomy, the second strand of human security that enables us to pursue meaningful participation in the processes that shape our lives, is also maximised in a capitalist market. Chapter 4 explains exactly why and how this argument is flawed when I turn to the issue of the public sphere and the role that the communications industries play within it. Significantly, the weaknesses of the prescriptive analysis of the good society that the neoliberal vision sets out follow on from the limitations of their analysis of how capitalist markets actually work in practice. A weak description of capitalist markets is followed by and connected to a weak prescriptive view of the good society. What is missing from neoliberal political economy in its analysis of states, capitalist markets and social groups is twofold: an understanding of political culture, and a substantive account of social power, coercion and interests. When these matters are addressed, the problems facing the neoliberal account of rationality, autonomy and choice are stark and we are left with quite a different and more realistic description of existing global social relations and their implications for human security.

CHAPTER 4

# Public Sphere, Private Power –
# The Limits to Autonomy
# and Human Security

## Developments in the Public Sphere

The Public Sphere is a realm between civil society and the
state, in which critical public discussion of matters of general
interest was institutionally guaranteed. The liberal Public
Sphere took shape in the specific historical context of a developing market economy. (Habermas, 1989: xi)

The concept of the public sphere and its relationship to the means
of communication has become a burgeoning area of research and
inquiry in contemporary analyses of global communication.
Although most often associated with the work of the German social
theorist Jürgen Habermas, the idea of the public sphere has its roots
in the Hellenic tradition and its concern with the establishment
and preservation of an arena where citizens can engage in the
substantive public issues of the day (Habermas, 1989). Habermas's
work has sought to transpose and revive those ideals in the context
of the rise of the modern mass (now global) media. The public
sphere is composed of a range of institutions that offer fora for
people to discuss, analyse, criticise and debate the existing social
order. In its modern origins in seventeenth- and eighteenth-century
Europe, these institutions took the form of coffee houses, libraries,
universities, new print media, and so on. The concept of the public
sphere in Habermas's work is tied in with classic Enlightenment
ideals about progress, free speech and the need for what Marx
famously called 'the ruthless criticism of all that exists'. In so doing
it was to be hoped that participation and later, democracy, would
triumph against authoritarian forms of governance and social
order. The premise is inherently libertarian.

For the public sphere to exist it requires the existence of diverse
and plural sources of information and communication, enabling
citizens to focus their attention upon the public issues that shape
their daily lives. Minimally, it requires that citizens not only listen
to but also are able to take part in the formation of public policy.
There is a wide debate here about the contested forms that democracy might take, from representative through to associational and

direct democracy (Held, 1987). What is not in doubt is that for the public sphere to be a substantive realm it cannot be dominated by any single institution or group of people. As Habermas argues, in its modern European form the major obstacle to enlightened inquiry was the power of the church, monarchy and state, all of whom had in part built their authoritarian power on the basis of the control of information, literacy and knowledge. Habermas's gloomy conclusion, very much in keeping with the Critical Theory school with which he is associated, was that the public sphere had been destroyed in modern industrial societies through the dramatically increased power of major private communications corporations to dominate the agenda-setting news media. Further, for Habermas this represents a refeudalisation of the public sphere by an unholy alliance of interests connecting the major media corporations with their respective state institutions who have sought to control the nature of political debate, campaigning and the flow of information in the public sphere.

Why, then, is this of concern for human security? The public sphere is vital to democracy and to human security precisely because it is about the promotion of human autonomy. In its ideal form, the public sphere is something approximating a neutral arena within which we can hope to reason about the issues that affect us in the public realm (O'Neill, 1995). Clearly this is an ideal and a host of other factors that inhibit reasoned analysis invariably come into play, such as inequalities of power in class, gender, ethnicity, and so on. None the less, if democracy is to be substantive in the modern world order then something like a range of public spheres that connects vast bodies of people over time and space must exist and must be defended (Schlesinger and Kevin, 2000). The way in which such public spheres are to be organised is, of course, open to debate and a range of possibilities. For Habermas, it was originally small-scale private organisations that provided the critical forum for questioning established authority. The irony for Habermas is that these private organisations eventually became the conglomerates that now dominate the public sphere and are no longer interested in openness, a plurality of voices or a critical analysis of everything that exists, least of all their own power and interests. However, as many critics have charged, Habermas's account overlooks the role played by working people in trade unions, book clubs, popular protests, and so on, in constructing the public sphere. Habermas's is largely an elite-driven view of the construction of the public sphere (Calhoun, 1992; McLaughlin, 1993; Durham Peters, 1993).

This duality is very important – it is easy, on reading Habermas's account, to view the public sphere as a realm constructed solely by the actions of aspirant bourgeoisie in newly industrialising Europe.

This would be a distortion of the complexities of social change in this period and the part played by working people. Indeed, as we will see in Chapter 6, there is a parallel between the early development of the public sphere and ongoing trends in the process and structure of globalisation in what I have elsewhere termed globalisation from above (GFA) and globalisation from below (GFB) (Wilkin, 2000).

The correct or necessary balance between centralised and decentralised control and ownership of the means of communication and its role in the public sphere(s) for modern democracy is not self-evident and will reflect a range of factors such as geography, population, technology, and so on. For example, Schlesinger and Kevin analyse this concept in the context of the European Union and the levels of public sphere that must exist in order to help establish a coherent European political culture (Schlesinger and Kevin, 2000). What is clear is that there are a variety of models for (the potential) organisation of these public sphere(s) available to us and the choices that are and have been made will reflect the realities of existing social power. Thus, as Andrew Davies has noted in his work on the organisation of telecommunications, perfectly good grounds exist for rejecting either capitalist markets or state-directed monopoly ownership of the telecommunications industry as the only choice available to us when considering the organisation of the means of communication (Davies, 1994). Davies sets out a persuasive case in favour of a decentralised model that is embedded in local and regional networks that are accountable democratically to their populace. The fact that this choice was not historically made in Britain is less to do with the rationality or practicality of the choice and everything to do with the interests of established political and economic institutions. All that is now left of the scheme for decentralised telecommunications in Britain is the independent region of Hull and Humberside, the subject of repeated and hostile takeover bids from private US corporations, and, interestingly, the Labour government's first partial privatisation in January 2000, illustrating the commitment to the neoliberal agenda of a socialist political party (Teather, 2000).

Clearly, given my overriding concern with issues of human security and the role that autonomy plays therein, the organisation of the public sphere(s) is a crucial issue in any society. In addition to this we must recognise that we are now talking about a public sphere that exists at a variety of levels: local, national, regional and global. My intention in this chapter is to examine the claims behind the neoliberal approach to the information society and its significance for the public sphere before arguing why the neoliberal approach is an inadequate mechanism for defending the public sphere. The failure of the neoliberal information society model is rooted in the criticisms, descriptive and prescriptive, that I laid out in the previous chapter and is part of its thin view of rationality and social power. Given the extended nature of the public sphere, this necessarily ties us into the issue of globalisation and I will turn to this in more detail in Chapter 6 when I look at the relationship between developing tendencies in globalisation, of which developments in the communication industries have played a key role. The idea of globalisation has clear implications for human security with its own global aspirations and what I will illustrate is the extent to which the main tendencies within it are compatible with the goal of human security. I want to begin by setting out the key principles of the information society that inform much of the neoliberal rhetoric about the impact of NIT on social order.

## *A Neoliberal Utopia? – The Information Society Considered*

The idea of the information society has its roots in modernist social and political thought that has sought to utilise technology as a means of liberating humanity from the drudgery of work. Implicit within this tradition of thought, that can be traced back at least to St Simon and Comte, has been the idea that organisational advances in industrial society would ultimately lead to a social order in which traditional causes of social conflict would become irrelevant (Wolin, 1961: Chapter 10). Class is the most obvious social category here but so too would be such concepts as patriarchy, race and nationalism. The technological breakthroughs of the past twenty-five years that have fuelled both the expansion of the role of the communications industry in the global (or 'new') economy and the restructuring of global capitalism and states alike have been central to the neoliberal vision of the information society (Reich, 1992; Moore, 1997; Gates, 1999). To reiterate, for the neoliberal the information society is the culmination of the good society within which the individual is freed by the extension of the marketplace into ever wider areas of life from which they can choose according to their own perceived wants and desires. There is no place for the concept of 'communication needs' in this view of the good society, as the concept of need is seen by many neoliberals as leading to authoritarian political practices. For the neoliberal, claims about needs are usually bound up with the role of the state in redistributing resources in society, ideally from rich to poor, under the pretext that the satisfaction of general needs has ethical priority over the liberty of the (rich) individual to spend their money as they please (Nozick, 1974; Friedman, 1978). Better, on neoliberal terms, to leave such questions of resource allocation to the individual to pursue their own chosen wants and desires. Ultimately we each know what is in our best interests. This is a complex issue and as this book progresses I will illustrate why the idea of 'communication needs' must be defended in any substantive account of human security, as it lies at the heart of the goal of general human autonomy. For now we can take it as read that for the neoliberal the idea of communication needs is at the very least a highly problematic concept.

So what does the idea of the information society mean to the neoliberal model of the good society? The very idea of a complex modern industrial society presupposes a high level of information flows between governments and citizens, companies and consumers, employers and employees; citizens in civil society and the new information technology (NIT) that we examined earlier comprise the infrastructure that makes this possible. The volume and speed of information flows fuelled by NIT has seen qualitative shifts in many areas of political and economic life world order. I want to deal with the major economic changes first.

## Economic Transformation

> The world's political structures are completely obsolete ... the critical issue of our time is the conceptual conflict between the global optimisation of resources and the independence of nation-states. (Jacques Maison Rouge, former IBM Chief Officer for European operations, in Mulgan, 1991: 220)

### Perfecting Market Transactions

To return to the quote from Maison Rouge is useful here as it illustrates a strong technocratic theme in neoliberal political economy. The technological transformation of global capitalism incorporating NIT and new managerial and working practices has produced a revolutionary transformation in economic organisation (Ohmae, 1990). However, while market practices are said to be moving towards the neoliberal ideal of perfectly functioning markets where demand meets supply (a truly rational world), our political structures are increasingly outdated. State intervention in the economy is said to have created a range of institutions and practices that inhibit the underlying potential of these economic developments and therefore needs to be fundamentally restructured. As various writers have noted this restructuring of state institutions and practices is well under way with the central emphasis upon privatisation, deregulation and the embedded principle of public subsidy for private profit (Gill, 1995; Wilkin, 1996). This has importance for human security and the communications industry as the idea of the means of communication as a public service intrinsic to a democratic order is eroded in favour of enhancing the power of privately owned and commercially driven institutions that are neither accountable to the public nor easily controlled by them. For the latter, communication is a commodity to be bought and sold. In addition to this, NIT enables firms to respond to changing patterns of demand in markets and to prepare the production and distribution of goods accordingly. Advanced and sophisticated forms of marketing are now utilised by any major corporation as a means of targeting potential customers and clients more specifically than ever before (Brown, 1995). Such developments depend upon the ability of companies to develop huge databases of information about individuals, households and other corporations from which they can project potential sales. As noted in Chapter 2, the Claritas Corporation has a database of over 500 million consumers. In turn consumers are said to receive more and better information than ever from which to make their choices. Thus the classical liberal economic goal of perfecting market transactions is fuelled by NIT developments.

*Global Markets?*
A second and related idea is that we are witnessing the emergence of truly global markets in which companies produce for a global consumer audience (Dicken, 1992 and 1998; Held, McGrew et al., 1999). Again, this idea has slipped into popular political discourse and no doubt has some degree of accuracy. Newly emerging mega communications conglomerates such as Disney/Capital Cities/ABC undoubtedly aim to capture as wide a global consumer audience as possible given the huge capital outlays involved in such products as contemporary Hollywood movies. However, (the idea of global markets is a gross oversimplification in that it fails to convey the hideously uneven nature of global trade which largely takes place between the world's three major economic blocs: roughly speaking, Japan, North America and the European Union (Bienefeld, 1996). Similar patterns also follow in terms of the flow of global investment, which is dominated by the core capitalist states and the most prominent states of the developing world such as China, Brazil and Argentina (Held et al., 1999: 243–51; *Economist*, 2000e; UNCTAD, 1999).

None the less, there is some substance to this idea of truly global markets. For example, developments in NIT have been crucial to the idea of global markets in which corporations no longer target particular nation-states or even regions but are able to produce goods and advertising for a (potentially) global audience. India, with an overall population of over one billion, has a burgeoning middle class of around 250 million people alongside the far greater proportion living in poverty. Comparative research reveals that advertising in India is following patterns similar to that found in the core capitalist states (Griffin et al., 1994).

New market possibilities are seen to be opened up by developments in NIT, with the Internet frequently described by politicians
and businesspeople alike as the major developing market place for
the twenty-first century. The concept of 'E-commerce' – electronic
business conducted through the Internet – has recently animated
the concerns of a number of core capitalist states and their corporations, all of whom are struggling to establish a grip upon what is
seen as the most important market in the new millennium. *The
Economist* has likened this development to a new economic and
political revolution, even allowing for the unstable nature of many
e-firms (*Economist*, 2000f, g and h). The most advanced sector of the
global market is arguably that of finance and investment. NIT
coupled with the deregulation of stock exchanges world-wide in
the 1980s has seen untrammelled volumes of capital flowing on a
global circuit chasing ever-higher returns on investment. To illustrate the significance of this, in 1971 around 90 per cent of
international financial transactions were related to what is referred
to as the real economy, trade or long-term investment, and 10 per
cent were speculative transactions. By 1990, the percentages were
reversed, and by 1995, as Chomsky notes, 'about 95% of the vastly
greater sums were speculative, with daily flows regularly exceeding
the combined foreign exchange reserves of the seven biggest industrial powers, over $1 trillion (US) a day, and very short-term: about
80% with round trips of a week or less' (Chomsky, 1999: 22–4).

There have, of course, been many spectacular stock market
collapses and financial disasters over the past twenty years but for
the thoroughgoing neoliberal this can usually be put down to the
*lack of* capitalist values and practices in those countries affected. For
example, the recent East Asian financial crisis has been attributed in
part to the problems generated by the lack of a commitment to the
kind of 'pure' free trade capitalism practised in the Anglo-American
model of development (*Economist*, 1998). The collapse of the East
Asian currencies was said to be in part a product of a kind of 'crony
capitalism' that had built up over a number of decades into a series
of very unsound economic practices. The collapse of the East Asian
currencies, while inducing hardship, would bring about much
needed reforms. Such an analysis fails to recognise that the emergence of authoritarian state-capitalist regimes in East and South-East
Asia in Indonesia, Thailand, Taiwan, South Korea, the Philippines
and Japan can only be understood if we recognise that the postwar
political economy of these states has been directly shaped by their
geopolitical relationship to the core capitalist bloc led by the United
States (Harris, 1986). Support for authoritarian and state-led capitalism in these states was of direct utility to the core capitalist bloc
in the Cold War era and it is a gross misreading to reduce the current
structure of political and economic organisation in these states to

differences of culture or so-called 'Asian values'. In the recent financial crisis, it was the vast capital flows from Western speculators
seeking quick and easy financial gain that originally fuelled the
unsustainable boom in countries that were, during the Cold War at
least, held up in the core capitalist states as models of successful
Third World development. As Doug Henwood notes, in the current
crisis it has been the combination of foreign capital *and* domestic
weakness that precipitated the crisis (Henwood, 1998a: 1). This
tendency of global capital has occurred in the US and Scandinavian
banking crises of the late 1980s and early 1990s, the European
monetary crisis of 1992, and Mexico's financial collapse in 1994–95
(Henwood, 1998b: 1)

*Restructuring the Workplace*
NIT in the workplace has transformed many production processes
on a number of levels. Apart from simply replacing much human
labour, NIT also enables companies to be flexible in their production
and terms of employment, enabling them to seek out the most profitable sites for production of goods and services (Sayer and Walker,
1992; Castells, 1998; Corbridge et al., 1994). In the years ahead it
seems likely that there will be an increasing tendency for the development of call centres and home-working in many industries in the
core states, further reducing costs to business of providing a place of
employment. Thus NIT has enabled corporations to reduce and
control labour costs in unprecedented fashion, as the threat of so-
called 'natural redundancy' hangs over workers in many industries.
    This disciplinary power of NIT in the workplace is, then, crucial
to neoliberal theory and practice. The dramatic rise in global unemployment that has taken place over the past two decades has in part
been an effect of the expanded use of NIT in the workplace. As
Robert Brady long ago recognised, the structure of large-scale private
enterprise tends to be totalitarian, with power flowing from the top
down towards employees who work in increasing levels of insecurity
(Brady, 1937). The majority of the workforce have little or no direct
control over the activities of their employer in terms of investment,
work conditions and so on. As a consequence, they are rendered
more vulnerable to the power and changing interests of capital.
    The attack upon independent trade unions, that has been a
persistent feature of the history of capitalism, has been intensified
since the early 1970s as capital has sought to reassert its power over
labour forces in the core capitalist states. It was in the core capitalist
states that workforces had most strongly been able to advance their
interests in the twentieth century, gaining an extension of political
and economic freedoms and resources that culminated in the varied
forms of welfare-state democracy that emerged around the world. It
is little surprise, then, that as the power of labour movements to

resist the transformations in global capitalism has waned so has the assault intensified upon the gains made by working and non-working people in terms of wages, welfare and public expenditure and cutbacks increased in many areas including trade union membership, and public spending on health and education (Hahnel, 1999, 6).[1]

*The Commodification of Information*
The commodification of information is seen as a progressive trend in neoliberal terms as it makes available to a wider market new forms of information and entertainment via NIT developments. For example, huge amounts of information can be contained on CD-ROM data-bases, and the growth of home computer ownership in the core capitalist states of the world is also a significant trend over the past twenty years. In theory and in practice consumers and citizens alike are able to pick and choose in the marketplace of information in order to find precisely what suits their particular interests. For companies, information is a source of economic power and the development of Trade-Related Intellectual Property Rights (TRIPs) over the course of the final (Uruguay) GATT Round has been very important for core capitalist states and their corporations. In practice this has enabled many core capitalist state corporations to take out patents on a range of goods, services and forms of information. Everything from seeds to human DNA is now open to the ownership and control of private corporations (*Third World Resurgence*, 1997).

The commodification of information is not, however, a new trend. For example, since the early 1960s Reuters, undoubtedly the world's most important and famous news agency, has made most of its profits from selling private economic information to companies that subscribe to their service (Boyd-Barrett and Rantanen, 1998: Chapter 5). However, the expanded realm of information commodi-fication has been dramatic in recent decades, with the steady erosion of a range of public forms of education and information from libraries to schools and broadcasting institutions. The neoliberal argument underpinning these changes is that it benefits consumers to have a wider variety of choices in a marketplace where increased consumption and competition lower the price of goods available, including information. In practice, as Herb Schiller noted, this is an idea that benefits the rich in general by encouraging governments to cut taxes that benefit the wealthy far more substantively than the poor and middle-income sections of society. Choice is only extended for those that can afford to pay. Where once information was freely available through education, broadcasting and libraries, increasingly charges are made. The divisions that this creates in society in terms of citizenship and participation should not be underestimated. Ultimately it deepens the tyranny of the minority (Schiller, 1989).

Having set out the major economic implications of NIT for the neoliberal vision of the good society let us now consider its political import. The lesson to be learnt here for the neoliberal is a familiar one: politicians and state institutions are to be treated with suspicion – they are not businesspeople and do not know how to run an economy.

### Political Transformation

### Revive Democracy

> '... the best way for a nation to make political decisions about its future is to empower all of its citizens to process the political information relevant to their lives and express their conclusions in free speech designed to persuade others ...' (Al Gore, quoted in Hacker, 1996: 213)

The connections between democracy, technology and Utopian social theory have long and deep roots in modernist thought as a number of writers have observed (Sclove, 1995; Beirne and Ramsay, 1992; McLean, 1989). The idea that technology and the rational organisation of society was a means to the end goal of a Utopia that would be in keeping with the 'end of ideology' thesis is a familiar refrain in writers from Huxley to Bell. [Technology would enable us to satisfy basic questions about material issues and at the same time NIT provides us with the possibilities for reviving practical and to some extent participatory democracy. The use of referendum, for example, is something that a number of politicians and writers have speculated could operate more widely at the local level (Hacker, 1996; Friedland, 1996). Given that the starting premise for the neoliberal view of society is the (abstract) rational, egoistic individual, then this offers great potential for enhancing individual liberty at the expense of the large-scale governmental and state bureaucracies that dominated so much of twentieth-century politics.

A range of actors, then, sees the utility of NIT, across the political spectrum of the core capitalist states, as having the potential to revive democratic participation. The issue of concern here for human security is directly to do with the theme of autonomy. NIT has multiple implications for political economy. It might well *potentially* have the capacity to enhance liberty and participatory democracy but its impact cannot be understood in isolation from the prevailing forms of social power that already exist in society. Indeed, *NIT also enhances the potential for industrial democracy* in which working people are able to exercise greater control over the resources and investments that are central to their human security (Sayer, 1995; Beirne and Ramsay, 1992; Albert and Hahnel, 1990).

However, NIT is introduced into social orders that are already structured by various institutions, procedures and social relations, and
its purpose cannot be seen in isolation from this. Whether or not
NIT will enhance participation and autonomy is a matter of social
struggle, it is not inherent to the technology itself.

*Increase the Power of Citizens*
A related theme for neoliberals and by way of extension the information society also means enhancing the power and ability of
individual citizens to act in political life. Citizenship can be
deepened and rendered more substantive via the use of NIT as it
provides citizens with the wide range of information that is necessary if they are to make rational political decisions (Friedland, 1996:
Sclove, 1995). While NIT provides the infrastructure through which
citizenship and governmental institutions can redraw their relationship, the global media as the Fourth Estate provides the plural,
open, diverse and critical forum within which important public
issues of the day can be addressed. A major concern of political
culture in the core capitalist states since the Second World War has
been the declining participation of electorates in electoral procedures and processes. It is argued that the enhanced role of the
citizen might well help to redress this imbalance by bringing
politics and the policy process back under the influence of the
general populace (Hacker, 1996). In an era where governing institutions are increasingly stretched through new regional and global
institutions such as the EU, NAFTA and the WTO, this is a potentially important aspect in the continuing legitimacy of
representative democratic processes. Such an assumption rests
upon a simple (not to say simplistic analysis) of electoral absten-
tions in core capitalist states, however. Turnouts for local elections
in Britain, for example, are as low as those for European
Parliamentary elections. None the less, the potential for enhancing
the power of citizens to shape and control the policy processes that
structure their lives is a factor that NIT brings us.

*Global Civil Society*
The idea of global civil society has become a buzzword for international relations theory and practice with writers, academics and
politicians alike drawing attention to what they see as an emergent
trend in world order (Walzer, 1995; Cox, 1999; Hague and Loader,
1999: 135–53). Given that civil society is probably the most
slippery of concepts in Western political thought, we should not be
too surprised to find that global civil society is a concept that is
both complex and has different meanings for different actors. I will
draw out this complexity in more detail in the remaining chapters
but here I want to adhere to the meaning of this term in the

context of the neoliberal framework that has shaped global political economy over the past few decades. For the neoliberal, global civil society is the realm of the entrepreneur, the agent of capital who takes the risks, speculates and innovates in a way that drives prosperity and progress. Hence we see the raft of global political economic policies advocated by neoliberal thought and now firmly entrenched via the 'Washington Consensus' and the major international financial institutions. Specifically, liberalisation, deregulation and privatisation have been devised with a view to enhancing the role of the entrepreneur, the private actor. In political terms, global civil society is said to be concerned with the spread of democracy and open government (Carrothers, 1999–2000). There will be no hiding place for dictators or repressive regimes in a global civil society where the global media can cast an almost continuous form of surveillance over the world's political actors (Habermas, 1999: 1–2). Thus, for the neoliberal there are two major strands to global civil society: the realm of economic entrepreneurial skill, and the realm where ordinary citizens and independent institutions such as the global media can survey and expose repressive regimes around the world in defence of democracy. As noted earlier, a number of writers have argued that the idea of global civil society is about a new form of global moral consciousness, shaped by the global media. Ordinary citizens are increasingly aware of their moral connections to oppressed peoples around the world and are able to use the NIT infrastructure and the global media to act in order to pressure governments to intervene over a range of places and issues, from famine to ethnic cleansing. Again, there is a strong link here between technology, democracy and morality as citizens around the world are able to extend their sense of moral obligation beyond the barriers of their own state and espouse the kind of internationalism that has been a feature of classical liberal thought.

## Conclusions: The Good Society?

All told, the neoliberal vision set out here is a powerful one and there is clearly much that even the ardent critic of neoliberal political economy would need to respond to. The information society is in many respects a reality that is both here and now, although vastly unevenly spread. The question that remains, then, is in two related parts: what does the information society mean for human security? And how should we evaluate the dominant neoliberal paradigm that is at the heart of the contemporary idea of the (global) information society? What I will show in the remaining chapters is that there are major problems with the view of the information society set out by neoliberal political economy that are precisely to do with the question of human autonomy that is a central feature of human security. As we have seen already, the information society for the neoliberal is about restructuring the relationship between government, citizens and corporations. In essence it defends the idea of private power leading to public good on the assumption that if you maximise people's free choices then you are most likely to realise the greatest happiness of the greatest number. After all, we invariably know what is in our best interests, don't we?

CHAPTER 5

# Building the Perfect Beast:
# The Information Society Revealed

Thus far I have set out the neoliberal model of the information society and its understanding of political economy. In this and the final chapter, I consider the problems that the neoliberal information society presents for human security, most significantly for the question of autonomy. A key question here is: *to what extent do existing institutional and procedural arrangements with regard to the ownership and control of the means of communication (at all four levels of world order: local, national, regional and global) support or provide obstacles to the satisfaction of human security in general and human autonomy in particular?* Human security depends upon the ability of people to establish or build upon the existing mechanisms that allow them to determine the public and private issues that structure existing social orders. In representative democracies, a range of electoral mechanisms enables citizens to participate at some level in the construction of the governing institutions and procedures that will shape the public policy that affects their lives. As we have seen, in theory, neoliberals and many others view the information society as offering us the potential for deepening and enhancing processes of meaningful democratic participation. Many aspects of the information society would seem to be of importance for human security and its concern with human autonomy as a key to attaining consensual social organisation. In this chapter I outline what I see as the fundamental weaknesses of the neoliberal case. It should not be assumed that this means that the information society itself does not have the potential to enhance human security in general, and human autonomy in particular. Clearly it does. While for some social theorists, technology itself is value-laden and problematic in its inception, encouraging some end goals rather than others, I do not think that this is the case with all technology (Shiva, 1987 and 1989). While it is difficult to argue that nuclear weapons have a multitude of potentially positive uses, with much of the new information technology (NIT) that we have focused upon it is clear that NIT's potential use is a more open-ended question. The ends to which NIT will be put will reflect the structure of power between state and governing institutions, capitalist markets and the institutions that dominate them, and the social groups that comprise any social order. NIT has a number of potential uses which could be employed for relatively libertarian or authoritarian ends.

To illustrate this point, the use of closed circuit television cameras (CCTV) in the UK has grown exponentially in the past decade and it is now seen by many councils as *de rigeur* in making towns and cities safer places to live. The argument is fairly simple: if people know that they are on camera then they will behave themselves, as they could be caught in the act of committing a crime. Aside from the problematic nature of video evidence itself, the simple causal argument presented to support the case for extending CCTV is far from certain. Significant evidence suggests that CCTV is not in any sense an inevitable success at crime prevention. For example, reports from Scotland and Wales assessing the impact of CCTV on crime have found that at best the evidence is inconclusive and that in many instances crime levels actually rose after CCTV had been introduced into areas (Seenan, 1999). The argument that CCTV enhances people's individual liberty and safety is problematic to say the least; instead we are left with the authoritarian implications of CCTV providing a form of state surveillance over society that would surely trouble any consistent libertarian. CCTV as an example of NIT has been introduced on the pretext that it enhances liberty, but in reality the evidence is mixed as to its impact upon crime. By contrast, it can equally be used as a mechanism for enhancing the power of the state over civil liberties, the very thing that consistent libertarians would abhor. My point here is that the critique of the neoliberal information society that follows is not premised upon the idea that NIT is inherently a bad thing. On the contrary, given human security's concern with general human development and autonomy, it is clear that technology has a potentially crucial role to play in this process. The problem with NIT as it stands is that its introduction raises a number of problems for human autonomy that can be analysed under two broad headings: the first is to do with the limits to the neoliberal political economy of communication; the second concerns the issues of rationality, social power and autonomy. I begin by focusing upon the first issue.

### The Public Sphere in the Information Age – Obstacles to Human Autonomy

The literature on citizenship is vast and growing all the time and I will not attempt to offer an overview of it here. It has taken something of a new twist in recent years because the ideas of global citizenship and global civil society have forced many to rethink the meaning of political obligation (Connolly, 1991). We are said by writers such as William Connolly, to live in an age when the nation-state as the primary reference point of political identity has run into a number of problems. Many citizens in the current world order no longer see themselves simply in terms of their national identity, but increasingly they act as global citizens. By this Connolly means that we are witnessing a transformation in global politics where citizens are able to join up with and coordinate their activities with people around the world on such issues as trade unions, the environment, human rights, religion and so on. NIT has provided a global infrastructure that allows for unprecedented levels of communication and coordination of activities not only by the state and corporate institutions that have constructed the framework and parameters of global civil society, but increasingly through the actions of ordinary citizens. Dramatic examples of this include the Zapatista uprising on 1 January 1994, emerging in protest at the coming into force of the North American Free Trade Agreement (NAFTA). More recently the protests at the World Trade Organization (WTO) summit in Seattle in late November and early December 2000 were organised primarily through the Seattle-based Direct Action Network and its use of the Internet (Wilkin, 2000). In the case of the Zapatistas, here was a modern guerrilla campaign that sought to present itself through the Internet in order to take advantage of global media interest. In addition to this, it sought to describe itself in internationalist terms as representing a variety of oppressed groups around the world fighting against a seemingly unstoppable global capitalism that was uprooting and impoverishing communities at the same time as it was accruing vast wealth for private institutions (Zapatistas, 1994; *NACLA*, 1994). My point here is to show that the meaning and practice of citizenship is becoming ever more complex as we enter the twenty-first century.

Of course, this should not be taken to mean that past examples of internationalist political movements such as communism, socialism, liberalism and so on, were not important. They were and in many respects clearly continue to be. What we are seeing, however, is a qualitatively new form of internationalism that can be carried out by relatively few people as well as vast numbers. This would seem to offer some succour to the concern with human autonomy expressed by human security. However, there are a number of problems with the idea of global citizenship that are directly to do with human autonomy and the means of communication that we need to draw out.

### Global Citizenship and Information Inequality

'Global communication is not universal communication.' (Mowlana, 1996: 195)

The first and perhaps most obvious obstacle to the idea of global citizenship is the deep forms of hierarchy and inequality that currently scar the world order. As the 1999 UN *Human Development Report* (among many other documents) notes, inequality takes a variety of forms around the world. Whilst the greatest degree of absolute poverty undoubtedly resides in Third World or peripheral countries, it is clear that both poverty and inequality are tendencies that integrate and shape all four levels of world order (local, national, regional and global), and that as social facts they are not primarily structured by nation-state boundaries (UNDP, 1999; World Bank, 2000; Thomas, 2000). With regard to the realm of information and communication, Mowlana's quotation is an apt one. Inequalities of information and communication have been a recurring feature of the rise of the current world order. They tend to take two forms: first, there is major inequality in the terms of the key political economy issue of who owns and controls the means of communication, the flow of information and communication and its content. Second is the question of what we might call the discourses of communication: who determines what constitutes news, information, the facts of the matter, the concepts, norms and values that go into the defining of history both distant and recent? This latter point is a concern with issues of power and knowledge and focuses upon the kind of themes and issues raised by Edward Said's work *Orientalism* (1978). The capacity to define what constitutes legitimate knowledge and information is not just a question of truthfulness but also one of social power. An extreme example of this occurs during wartime as recent events in the Gulf and the former Yugoslavia illustrate, when powerful Western governments sought to utilise the tools of propaganda in order to set out a version of events that would help to legitimise their actions (Knightley, 1999 and 2000).

Mowlana's point is an important one, as it illustrates one of the central problems facing those who would defend the idea of global citizenship. The idea of citizenship bestows formal rights and obligations upon all citizens – rights and obligations that are said to be shared equally (Plant, 1988; Vandenberg, 1999). However, in practice, equality of citizenship is a misnomer in a world marked by overwhelming hierarchies and inequalities: between nation-states, between classes, men and women, citizens, states and corporations, and so on. As we have already noted, the public sphere is no longer a realm that simply occurs within a given nation-state but is one shaped by governing institutions that exist at all four levels of world order. For citizens to be meaningful participants in the multi-levels of this global public sphere requires access to an array of tools and resources, among the most important of which are the ability to communicate with others. Developments in global communications technology are complex and contradictory but there is little reason to doubt that they have been used by the dominant states, classes and corporations to enhance and maintain their own positions of power and authority. For example, the now (temporarily) suspended Multilateral Agreement on Investment (MAI) would have enshrined in international and enforceable trade agreements the premise that corporations are entitled to the same kind of rights as individuals (Thomas, 2000: 86–7). In practice, this would have dramatically enhanced the power of private companies over democratically elected governments. Private and unaccountable power would increase at the expense of democracy. This also raises the question of uneven access to and influence over the public sphere. Given that the idea of a public sphere can now be seen to connect us in a local, national, regional and global framework, it is quite clear which actors have the greatest reach in this multi-layered realm. Microsoft, British Telecommunications Plc and News Corporation, to name three examples, all have immense resources and power as private institutions to shape the structure and agenda of the public sphere at a variety of levels. The private power of corporations is out of all proportion to the ability of ordinary citizens, even when formed in collective groups such as trade unions, to influence the policy process. A good example of this imbalance was illustrated by newly elected Prime Minister Tony Blair's intervention on behalf of Rupert Murdoch's News Corporation in Italy in 1998 when he raised the possibility of News Corporation gaining greater access to the Italian media market with then Italian Prime Minister Prodi (BBC News, 1998). This was all the more extraordinary an act for a British Labour Prime Minister to be undertaking given Rupert Murdoch's demonic status in Labour Party history.

Global citizenship is an important theme for human security precisely because it is, in part, a universal claim about human dignity and autonomy. It is important to the human security debate because it does emphasise the complexity and interwoven nature of the four levels of world order. In theory, it offers a concept through which some kind of global consensus about rights, obligations and participation in the processes that shape public policy might be agreed. A key to the possibility of global citizenship is undoubtedly the dramatic changes in the means of communication that we have focused on throughout this book. As we will see in Chapter 6, evidence suggests that we are witnessing a substantive and qualitative change in world order that is in some part driven by actors acting as global citizens. However, we need to recognise the structural and institutional inequalities that shape world order and nowhere are these more evident than in the field of communications. As Schiller and others have noted, if anything the private control of information and the means of communication have intensified in the past two decades, a factor we focused upon in Chapter 2 (Schiller, 1989).

To illustrate the nature of these information and communication inequalities, the UN *Human Development Report* for 1999 focuses upon the uneven spread of NIT as we move into the twenty-first century. The expansion of global communication over the past two decades is seeing a general tendency towards increased telephone use, the spread of computer-driven telecommunications networks both public and private, and the expansion of such tools as the Internet. However, unsurprisingly the 1999 *Report* illustrates just how uneven this process remains with the core capitalist states largely leading the way in the ownership and control of global communications products (UNDP, 1999: Chapter 2).

What these tendencies reveal is the widely uneven spread of NIT and telecommunications between nation-states but, as we have also noted, it reveals the inequality within nation-states. Hence we need to view these tendencies in terms of the four levels of world order rather than simply as being comparisons between discrete nation-states. We are left with a complex pattern of communication haves and have-nots that unsurprisingly reflects most strongly the power of the core capitalist classes and states. However, there is also a significant and growing wealthy strata of population in many of the major developing countries such as Brazil, China, India, Argentina, Mexico, South Africa and South Korea, who are all part of this framework (Mohammadi, 1997).

*Media Autonomy*
The public sphere of the social democratic welfare state is a field of competition among conflicting interests, in which organisations represent diverse constituencies, negotiate and compromise among themselves and with government officials, while excluding the public from their proceedings. (Habermas, 1989: xii)

The independence of the media has been a key theme in Western political thought since the French Revolution. The Fourth Estate, as it has subsequently become known, was to act as an independent force in society, scrutinising the actions of those with political power in order to inform ordinary citizens when abuses of authority occurred (Unger, 1991; Keane, 1991). Indeed, this idea fits in with Habermas's account of the early years of the modern Public Sphere in which privately owned and run newspapers were seen to be the fora for wide, though not universal, public debate on important political issues of the day. Most research tends to conclude that people gain their information about politics, the economy and society from the mainstream news media, and overwhelmingly from broadcast rather than print media. It is crucial, therefore, that the information they receive is not simply an expression and defence of the interests of those actors and institutions who already possess political and economic power. There is a

deep and wide-ranging literature on just this topic, much of it
critical, and it is not my intention here to set out an elaborate thesis
on the limits of the media's autonomy as actors in global communication (Herman and Chomsky, 1988; Altschull, 1995; Garnham,
1990; Golding and Murdock, 1977). Rather it is sufficient, I think,
to show that there are major structural and ideological obstacles to
the autonomy of the mainstream global communication corporations with regard to political and economic power. These obstacles
are both general and particular and how they manifest themselves
in any given time and place will reflect the interplay of the broad
structural tendencies and the contingent local, national or regional
factors. A generalisable model of the media *per se* that allows for
predictions of outcomes or media behaviour is not a realistic goal
for social science, but what we can aspire to do is locate the broad
structural tendencies that operate at a general level and within
which all global communications corporations have to exist.[1] From
this it is possible to look at concrete examples of media institutions
within specific local, national, regional and global settings, taking
into account the array of contingent and particular factors that
have helped to shape media practices in different nation-states and
regions. Dealing with the general tendencies first we can focus
upon the two major structuring tendencies that have served to
shape the modern world order:

## Communications Corporations in the Inter-State System

As I wrote earlier in the book, the two major structuring factors of
the modern world order can be seen as global capitalism and the
modern inter-state system. Dealing with the latter first, the inter-
state system of nation-states has historically provided a primary
form of social and political identity to particular populations. The
mythical qualities of nationalism, in part built up through the
means of communication both traditional (oral) and modern
(print/electronic/ocular), have proven to be crucial building blocks
in the modern world order. The rise of modern nation-states in all
of their diverse forms since the seventeenth century in Europe has
been accompanied by the attempts of state institutions to regulate,
to a greater or lesser degree, the means of communication. The
strong, historic relationship between the nation-state and the
means of communication, from telecommunications through to
news media, is a central part of the political economy of communications and has provided a major constraint on the autonomy of
the media. All state institutions, irrespective of type, have had and
continue to have some means of constraining media activity,
whether through the issuing of licenses, the taxation of publications, or various tools of censorship, usually under the pretext of
national security. In addition, states remain primary sources of

information for news agencies and journalists alike, giving them potential leverage over the presentation of news issues (Seymour-Ure, 1996: Chapters 8–10; McManus, 1994). As we have seen in Chapter 2, modern global communications media have been reliant upon state institutions to act on their behalf in major trade agreements to bring about the kind of economic changes that they have tended to advocate. This is not to suggest that the interests of state actors and institutions are simply reducible to those of global communications corporations. On the contrary, what it does reveal is the symbiotic nature of the relationship between the two. Far from being autonomous of state institutions, the global communications corporations need state institutions to protect and promote their interests. Recent examples of these co-dependent relationships between communications corporations and state institutions can be seen in the ongoing battle in the United States over the monopolising power of Microsoft in the computer software market, where an inter-capitalist dispute has led to the state being forced to intervene in order to ensure that a wider range of capitalist companies and their elites are able to exploit the expanding global computer software market. In addition we have also had in Europe examples of European governments acting to regulate and protect domestic media companies from US competition, with France being the most consistently vociferous promoter of this line (Hamelink, 1997; Tomlinson, 1997).

*Communications Corporations and Global Capitalism*
The second major constraint upon global communications corporations is equally transparent. By and large they are major capitalist corporations, driven by the objective need to make a profit, not to provide a public service or satisfy some notion of communication needs that might, in turn, enable meaningful global citizenship. The fact that they are capitalist corporations brings with it a range of structural and ideological constraints upon the media's autonomy. In ideological terms, as capitalist corporations they bring with them and defend a particular set of values and beliefs. They are not the neutral arenas of liberal belief but are intrinsically pro-capitalist institutions. As Herman and McChesney have recently commented the global media are the 'new missionaries of corporate capitalism' (Herman and McChesney, 1997). There are, quite simply, no global communications corporations in existence that are in favour of socially owned and/or managed approaches to the means of communication. This does not mean that there cannot be dissent and criticism of existing institutions, on the contrary, criticism is a necessary feature of any way of life if it is not to stagnate. However, it does set limits on the kinds of criticism that we are likely to experience. In ideological terms, the defence of capitalism is a base line

for any of these global corporations and this is no surprise. In structural terms, global capitalism constrains the autonomy of the media
because it forces them to pursue profit first and foremost.[2] The
commitment to corporate capitalism and the neoliberal policy
agenda is presented as a kind of natural good for all people, above
and beyond mere political ideology, a policy agenda based upon
essential truths about the way in which the world is. As Trevor
Kavanagh, the political editor of Britain's most popular tabloid the
*Sun* has commented about his newspaper's political loyalties, 'we are
for good economic management, small government, small taxes,
law and order and a strong defence' (Greenslade, 2000a). The impli-
cation here is clear, as a capitalist communication corporation the
*Sun* will support whichever political party endorses its own policy
agenda. As a powerful capitalist institution, this is a perfectly logical
position to take: private capitalist institutions promote their own
interests, not the publics. Thus when the *Sun* switched support from
the Conservative Party to the Labour Party at the 1997 British
general election it wasn't, as Kavanagh notes, 'such a dramatic
change to support Blair', primarily because the incoming Labour
administration were largely committed to a policy agenda that
reflected the interests of corporate capitalism (Greenslade, 2000a).

Profit for modern global media comes primarily through
accruing advertising revenue (Herman and McChesney, 1997:
58–65). There is little evidence to suggest that global media corporations will be successful in doing this if they base their activities
on a persistently critical examination of the activities of corporations upon whose advertising revenue they depend. Indeed, taking
this issue further, given the ways in which most global communications corporations are vertically and horizontally integrated with
a range of other companies and industries, they might even be
placed in the position of investigating and exposing their own
wrongdoing. The rise of Silvio Berlusconi as both an Italian media
mogul and major politician is an extreme though perhaps unsurprising illustration of the implications of the ever more complex
connections between political and corporate interests (Carroll,
2000). Equally one can look at the more 'benign' examples of the
ways in which cross-media ownership links diverse corporate interests in ways which would seem to dramatically refute the liberal
model of the media as a Fourth Estate, free of vested interests, open-
minded and critical. The acquisition of Star television by News
Corporation in order to broadcast into China is another good
example of this. The most decisive act of News Corporation when
taking over the Star satellite was to remove the BBC news coverage
that had caused offence to the ruling regime in China because of its
critical analysis of China's human rights record (Herman and
McChesney, 1997: 74–5). There is, then, an inherent tension and

contradiction between the idea of media corporations acting as the Fourth Estate, in some kind of public interest role, and their interests as private actors in a capitalist market seeking to accrue profits. The two cannot easily be reconciled. These are the two major general structural tendencies that constrain the autonomy of the global media. There are substantial material and ideational obstacles that serve to constrain and enable the things that communications corporations can do. Primarily they are operating under the twin pressures of global capitalism (the pursuit of profit) and the inter-state system (the national interest).[3] These twin structural properties help to define what policies both companies and state institutions alike will pursue. As Ben Bagdikian has noted, private companies and private power generally have a variety of mechanisms through which to exert influence over the media and its programming. Major advertisers have insisted that any of the following be included in corporate programming:

> All businesses are good or, if not, are always condemned by other businesses. All wars are humane. The status quo is wonderful. Also wonderful are grocery stores, bakeries, drug companies, restaurants and laundries. Religionists, especially clergy, are perfect. All users of cigarettes are gentle, graceful, healthy, youthful people. In fact, anyone who uses tobacco products is a hero. People who commit suicide never do it with pills. All financial institutions are always in good shape. The American way of life is beyond question. [Bagdikian, 1992: 154]

In a way, though, Bagdikian's example is beside the point. These are, after all, capitalist institutions. As such it would be surprising if they wanted to see any other values expressed in media that they were effectively sponsoring.

## Theoretical Considerations

Moving from the general to the particular we can draw out a range of contingent and concrete factors that can affect the autonomy of the media in different times and places. These factors should be viewed always in relation to the position of the media institutions within the specific nation-state and/or regional framework with which we are concerned and its historical emergence in the modern world order. I mention this only because to talk simply in terms of internal and external factors is misleading as it implies that particular states might somehow have been outside the twin systems of global capitalism or the inter-state system. This is not possible as the nature of modern nation-states needs to be understood always in relation to the general and the particular. *States are both part of world order and yet distinctive within it, not separate from it.*

*State History/Typology*
As writers such as Immanuel Wallerstein, Charles Tilly, Barrington
Moore and Theda Skocpol have argued, there have been and
continue to be different *types* of states in the modern world order
and they can be typologised in a number of different ways and on
different scales. For example, states can vary between democratic
and undemocratic, more authoritarian and less authoritarian, more
developed and less developed, theocratic and secular, and so on.
The particular histories of different nation-states will be significant
features in the form that their particular local, national and
regional communications systems and institutions take. However,
these local developments must be seen in the wider national,
regional and global context in which they have emerged. For
example, as Hamid Mowlana has shown with the rise of modern
communications in Iran, this has been influenced both by local
and national characteristics as well as Iran's historical relationship
to the dominant Western, modernising forces of world order
(Mowlana, 1996).

*Political Culture*
The political culture of a particular nation or region refers, in this
sense, to a particular form of political life: the institutions,
processes and procedures that shape and structure it, and the
dominant values and beliefs about the system (Schlesinger and
Kevin, 2000: 210). Political institutions might be more or less
tolerant of media autonomy, in either an overt or a covert way. A
cursory study of an issue of the journal *Index on Censorship* reveals
the ways in which different nation-states impose often deadly overt
constraints upon the activities of journalists and newspapers
around the world. This is a global phenomenon, not something
that occurs simply in developing countries. The autonomy of the
media to investigate, present critical analyses and provide an open
forum for contrasting social and political viewpoints does not
simply reflect the overt power of state institutions to suppress or
intimidate, it also reflects the capacity of capitalist markets to
censor issues. The idea of market censorship is an important issue
as invariably capitalist markets are described as 'free' markets when
in truth they are, as we have seen, far from being free. Market
censorship takes a number of forms but here are two well-docu-
mented examples. First, the need to attract advertising revenue by
media companies is seen by a number of commentators as serving
to stifle political diversity in news media. The reason for this is that
advertisers are less likely to choose to advertise in papers, radio or
TV fora that might be overly critical of either their own particular
institution or of capitalism in general (Evans, 1998; Curran and
Seaton, 1997; Bagdikian, 1992). Second, the culture of a newsroom

is important in defining the parameters of what are and are not acceptable topics for coverage, the language used in covering an issue, where stories are to occur in a newspaper or broadcast. Again, many writers and journalists have reflected upon this form of self-censorship that becomes, in effect, a format for the production of news that structures editorial and journalistic practices (Negrine, 1996: 65; McManus, 1994).

*Material Resources*
Finally, material resources are crucial in the autonomy of particular media institutions. These resources include not only human resources from journalists to technical staff, but also such factors as the time and the space necessary to cover particular topics. Clearly there is no real comparison between a global actor such as CNN, now part of the Time-Warner empire, and the activities of even the largest media actors in the developing world such as the Brazilian Globo in terms of depth of coverage, global reach, access to major political and economic actors, audiences and institutions, and so on. Thus, the activities of the global media corporations are qualitatively on a different plane to those of even large-scale nationally based print and electronic media institutions. This is reflected not only in the relations between global communications corporations of the core nation-states and those of the developing world but is also a factor in the relations between core states. A great deal of the regional and local print media in Britain is now owned by a handful of major communications actors. For example, Newsquest, owner of around 190 titles in the UK, is itself a subsidiary of the US company Gannett, which has 74 titles running across the US (Greenslade, 2000b). What these factors reveal are the limitations on the liberal ideal of the news media as neutral or autonomous actors. The gathering of information by media institutions is overwhelmingly structured towards sources provided by states, private companies and public relations firms (McManus, 1994; Jackall, 1995). Robin Jackall and Janice Hirota quote a news source who claims that 'P.R. practitioners generally estimate that 80% of news is "placed news" in either print or electronic media' (Jackall and Hirota, 1995: 149). This is not to say that the idea of a neutral space in public life where public issues can be addressed is not in itself to be defended. As John O'Neill has written in an important article on this theme, the possibility of progressive social and political change, including, I would argue, the attainment of global human security, depends in part upon the construction of just such an arena (O'Neill, 1995). I want to turn now to the next sphere of criticism of the neoliberal information society and how it potentially and in practice curbs and limits human autonomy as a factor of human security.

## Democracy against Capitalism? The Neutered State

In neoliberal terms, there is a strong link between capitalism, democracy and peace, a theme that has run through the resurgence of liberal internationalist thought in international relations. For many writers, world order is moving slowly but surely towards the values and ideals of liberal capitalist democracy precisely because it is these that are said to provide the most people with the greatest degree of personal liberty and material comfort in human history (Fukuyama, 1992: Part V; Little, 1995). There is little reason to doubt the productive capacity of corporations under capitalism, but from a human security perspective the above neoliberal triad of capitalism, democracy and peace fails to address and understand some of the most significant developments of the global information society. Three main tendencies are developing in world order that go to the heart of the idea of human autonomy and which raise important questions about the relationship between capitalism and democracy. As I discussed earlier, the possibility of human autonomy ultimately presupposes some kind of democratic system, though what form democracy might take is a question open to a range of possible answers. What the information society reveals, in practice, is a series of important questions about the structure of power that exists between states, corporations, groups and citizens in world order. Again, we are dealing with both general tendencies and particular or contingent factors in explaining this but what becomes reasonably clear here is *that there is no necessary relation between capitalism and democracy* (Woods, 1995). Indeed, when one considers the historical emergence of capitalism around the world it has invariably been either prior to the emergence of what we take to be democracy or has frequently been something imposed upon the general populace at the expense of meaningful democracy or self-determination. Given that capitalism is, for neoliberals, a rational choice, there has been a great deal of resistance to its introduction throughout history, as Karl Polanyi has famously described (Polanyi, 1944). Turning to the first of the two general tendencies that are central to the information society I want to consider the changing structure of state–corporate relations in world order.

### The Neutered State and Vulture Capitalism

Developments in NIT have clearly empowered the world's major corporations, media included, with regard to their ability to pressurise governments around the world to pursue policy agendas that reflect their interests. Thus we have seen a movement towards the 'Washington Consensus' which promotes low taxation, low growth, low public spending, privatisation, deregulation and liberalisation of trade, largely where it suits the interests of the world's core capitalist states and their corporations (Cavanagh et al., 1994: 3). The enhanced mobility of capital has empowered corporations and investors alike to pressurise all governments that wish to be a part of the global economy to pursue something like this clutch of policies. Hence, we have seen that in such disparate economies as those of Eastern Europe, Russia, the recently collapsed Far East and South East Asia, economic chaos has led to the extension of various parts of this orthodox bundle of neoliberal policies as means for 'rescuing' these economies. In practice, what this represents is a significant and qualitative shift of power away from public and into private hands. As state institutions retreat from areas that were previously their domain, they are handing power over to private companies who have no particular responsibility to the public and are not directly accountable to them. Indeed, when working people do try to resist such policies they are invariably met with a welter of anti-trade union policies that are also a feature of the 'Washington Consensus' (Thomas, 2000: 39–46).

Most significantly, state power over the economy with a view to directing resources towards the satisfaction of human needs is severely constrained by neoliberal orthodoxy, as Herb Schiller has made clear in his devastating study, *Culture Inc.* (1989). In this work Schiller focuses upon the growing privatisation of information and what were previously public resources. This trend, global and spreading, ultimately represents an undermining of democracy and general autonomy because it takes available resources and places them in the hands of private actors and institutions. In practical terms, it entrenches hierarchies of social power by privileging the capacity of those with the necessary resources to have greater access to and control over the means of communication and the production of information. In a capitalist market economy, if you can't pay for them then you won't have access to them and the kinds of social hierarchies and inequalities that we have already focused upon become even more embedded.[4] The trends we are witnessing in the current global information society do a great deal to reinforce private power at the expense of autonomy and democracy. When it comes to public expenditure on welfare, health, education and literacy, we are in the presence of the *neutered state*, vulnerable and open to the pressures of the global market (Merrien, 1998). In truth, this often means states being pressurised by the capitalist institutions and actors who choose to attack governments who fail to adhere to their version of fiscal orthodoxy. This has happened to weak and powerful governments alike, from Mexico to the United Kingdom to Sweden.

The information society differentially empowers corporations and investors through its technological infrastructure that enables them to relocate investment and capital at hitherto unprecedented speeds. It allows private and unelected corporations to exercise, to a greater or lesser degree, undue control and influence over public policy, a perverse inversion of democracy. A good example of this is the aforementioned WTO structure as revealed at Seattle, where corporations 'sponsored' the event in return for varying degrees of access to representative ministers (see Chapter 3). This power is exerted by capitalist corporations and investors who, in a global economy structured to ease their freedom of movements and enhance their own power as actors, can use their mobility to pressurise governments into adopting the correct raft of neoliberal policies. This remains a question of political power and struggle, of course, and there is nothing inevitable about the outcomes that ensue as a result of this corporate power. But it does place severe constraints on elected governments and populations alike.

The rational choice in the current corporate capitalist world order is as follows: if you are a political party, adopt the range of neoliberal policies that corporate interests would like to see and you have a better chance of gaining their support; fail to do so and you will gain their opposition which might take the form of the threat of disinvestment or in the case of media companies, political attacks in the press. The case of the German finance minister Oskar Lafontaine is a good example of the latter. Lafontaine came into office with the Social Democratic government in Germany in 1998 and soon came under strong attack from significant sections of the media across Europe for his avowed European Federalist ambitions and the defence of a modest form of economic Keynesianism. In essence, Lafontaine's error was to call for government-led stimulation of demand by either a reduction of interest rates across Europe or increased government spending (*Business Week*, 1998b). Lafontaine's ideas were seen as a threat by the business community in Europe and elsewhere, leading *The Economist* to ask, 'Who really runs Germany?' (*Economist*, 1998a). Sustained pressure on Lafontaine from sections of the European media, business and even nominally allied parties such as the British Labour government, led to his eventual resignation in March 1999. Lafontaine's modest Keynesian goals were clearly too much for capitalist investors and companies alike to bear and, as if to illustrate the power of capital to tame the fortunes of politicians and governments, the news of his resignation led to a surge in share prices in the Frankfurt stock exchange (BBC News, 1999a). For the electorate the lesson here is clear. The rational choice is to support the party that supports corporate capitalist interests. Of course, you have a choice not to do so, but if you elect a government committed to the wrong policies, you will suffer the consequences accordingly.

The impact of these threats of disinvestment, economic instability and attack by currency speculators will vary in accord with a particular state's position in the structure of world order; none the less it illustrates the extent of the power of corporate capitalist interests to shape policy and regulation for their own ends and at the expense of the public interest and social need. After all, in a democracy the government is primarily there to represent the interests of the public, not of private companies.

A good example of this can be seen in one of the largest economies of the developing world, that of Brazil. The 1980s and 1990s have seen a number of fiercely contested presidential contests between the Worker's Party (PT) and the mainstream Party of the Liberal Front (PFL), Party of the Brazilian Democratic Movement (PMDB) and the Social Democratic Party of Brazil (PSDB). The Worker's Party have been represented by the well-known trade unionist Luis 'lula' da Silva and have espoused policies that addressed issues of welfare, education, health care rights for the poor, all of which go very much against the grain of the neoliberal agenda. In elections in 1989, 1994 and 1998, the Worker's Party was attacked mercilessly by Brazil's independent TV Globo who invariably, in an independent and rational manner, sided with the parties of big business (Keck, 1992b: 24–9, 1992a; Sader and Silverstein, 1991; *NACLA*, 1995).[5] Despite the fact that the parties of big business have been exposed as being hideously corrupt, forcing the resignation of one president, they still remain the rational choice in an era of neoliberal global governance.[6]

Provided that you understand the first principles here, which are that profit and power for private companies are the ultimate public good, then you can make the right choices. If you fail to understand this then there are a variety of mechanisms for bringing you around to the right way of thinking, as countries as far apart as Vietnam and Haiti have found in the 1980s and 1990s. This is not to say that democratic processes under liberal capitalism are meaningless, far from it. It is merely to illustrate their (potential and actual) limitations as procedures. In practical terms, it is clear that much progress has been made in Brazil by political and social movements seeking to challenge the existing structure of political-economic power and *in part* this has come about through the success of the Worker's Party (among others) in national elections. *The formal procedures of democracy are not irrelevant to social change.* Nor, however, is there a straightforward relationship between them. The movement towards progressive social change of the kind that animates anti-systemic movements will reflect the relationship between systemic properties of global capitalism and the inter-state system as well as the particular and concrete circumstances of specific places (Arrighi et al., 1989). Indeed, given that formal democracy has only really been re-established in Brazil since the 1980s after nearly twenty years of brutal military dictatorship, the growth of social and political movements around human rights, peasants' rights, gender equality, and other anti-systemic issues has been remarkable (Rodrigues, 1995; Tavares, 1995).

To return to the theme of the relationship between the 'information society' and the state, it must be stressed that the point here is not to suggest that the state in all of its diverse types has simply been hollowed out by the information society. As I have said earlier, a state's relationship to capital has been restructured so that state power is still substantive and crucial in areas that support private power, but it is weakened in areas that promote general public good. The impact of these tendencies will vary in practice according to the location of particular states in the structure of power that is world order; following Wallerstein, whether states are in the core, the semi-periphery or the periphery. What we see here is the legitimisation of a form of welfare for the rich and powerful. At the same time, however, it is clearly *quite wrong* for the government to subsidise the things that would benefit the population in general, such as ensuring free higher education for all. The fact that governments can afford one but not the other says a great deal about the structure of social power and values that currently exist between states, social groups and corporations in the global information society. What the global information society has led to is a form of *vulture capitalism* that sees investors and corporations alike able to pursue their private interests in ever more speedy and socially disastrous ways for working and non-working people. The relationship between capital and labour is ever more akin to that of a predator and, at present, a comparatively defenceless and vulnerable prey waiting to be devoured. I want to turn now to the relationship between corporations, states and citizens in the global information society.

*Global Surveillance and Human Security*

At the heart of the neoliberal vision of the information society, a glaring and powerful contradiction troubles liberals and non-liberals alike. NIT provides the means for enhancing the responsiveness of corporations to changing patterns of consumer demand as well as more advanced means for attempting to shape those patterns of consumption through niche marketing, targeting of consumers, and so on. By surveying markets more acutely than ever before, companies can respond immediately to changing conditions and circumstances. But the notion of surveillance raises as many problems for the citizen as it is said to bring benefits to the consumer. In truth, these are never two separate categories. Corporations and state institutions alike are building up huge databases of information on individuals and households at all levels. For companies this is premised on the basis of being able to match production more directly to consumer tastes. For state institutions it is to enhance security and prevent crime within a given territory. At the same time, however, these trends raise dramatic problems for human autonomy. While the consumer gains information, citizens are having their civil liberties, most obviously the right to privacy, eroded. For example, within the European Union, developments are in place to standardise policing practices and operations across the European Union. As various civil liberties organisations have pointed out, there is comparatively little concern with the implications of these trends for civil liberties in the EU (Walker, 1999; *Economist*, 1999; Statewatch homepage, 2000).

Equally, in the workplace, the introduction of NIT has a number of draconian implications for workers. NIT is often a mechanism for replacing workers or deskilling, with the machine taking over the more complex tasks. The result of this is invariably an attack on the pay and conditions of the remaining workers who are vulnerable to enhanced workplace discipline. NIT is also used in the workplace to monitor the activities of individual workers in order to measure and quantify their efforts (*Economist*, 1999; Sayer and Walker, 1992). This is a feature of both traditional blue-collar industries and white-collar industries and works in part by imposing self-discipline upon the workforce. NIT is not simply a mechanism for empowering the citizen at the expense of the state and corporations. Both public and private institutions alike are also dramatically empowered by NIT in their capacity to control and discipline citizens, workers and consumers. The contradiction here in the neoliberal view of the information society is that the spread of information does not simply empower citizens, it also disproportionately empowers major public and private institutions and erodes the privacy and autonomy of the individual and social groups. To reiterate a basic point, NIT is not a neutral process. How it is introduced and for what purpose will reflect the prevailing and complex structures of power between global capitalism, global social forces and geopolitical institutions, as was illustrated in Figure 2.1. Where, then, does this leave human security and the issue of autonomy?

## Human Security, Autonomy and the Information Society

The idea of the information society certainly contains the seeds for enhancing human security, both in terms of need satisfaction and autonomy and the institutional infrastructure that might support this. NIT qualitatively improves our capacity to organise production and the distribution of goods and services so as to meet the general and particular needs of distinct groups and individuals, in theory at least. However, what we see in practice are the contradictions that abound between citizen and consumer, employer and employee, states and citizens, classes, and so on. While NIT offers the potential to extend human autonomy and make the public sphere a reinvigorated realm at a complex array of analytically distinct but related levels (local, national, regional and global), at the same time under existing hierarchies of world order it also has the tendency to deepen inequalities of social power. This process of application is ongoing and unfolding. For the moment, the public sphere in the information age remains a site of conflict and contestation around a series of contradictions that run like faultlines through the structure of power between the states, capital and social groups. Having set out the limitations of the neoliberal political economy of the information society, I can now turn to the second major flaw in the neoliberal approach to the public sphere and that concerns the issues of power, rationality and autonomy.

### Rational Choices and Autonomy in the Age of Private Power

The neoliberal model of the good society that has become the orthodoxy in global political economy is an inadequate one for attaining human security, that much is clear. Its weaknesses are both descriptive/explanatory in terms of how the information society actually works in practice but also conceptual in terms of how it views questions of power and rationality. What I will show in this section is that the neoliberal model presents us with thin accounts of both rationality and power that are so abstract as to be of limited use to us in explaining the concrete actions of individuals, groups and institutions in any given place. This descriptive/explanatory weakness also helps to explain why there is also a prescriptive weakness in the neoliberal view of the good society. There are two major issues that I will address here concerning: political culture and ideology.

### The View from Nowhere? – Rationality, Autonomy and Political Culture

A fundamental weakness in the neoliberal vision of human autonomy and rational choices is that it is a violently abstract account of human agency. By this I mean that it presents us with an account of the rationally choosing, egoistic individual who thinks, chooses and acts as though in an arena where they are able to take a neutral assessment of the world around them. Whilst I do not remotely agree with the chorus of social theorists who deny the possibility of objectivity in social inquiry, none the less it is important to recognise that there are major problems with the neoliberal account of the (hyper) rational actor. When we make judgements and develop analyses about the natural or the social world we are not making observations from outside our culture and history: the view from nowhere. On the contrary, our analyses are always from somewhere, they are always developed from within and against a concrete social and historical context: the view from somewhere. It is my contention that this 'view from somewhere' means that we must reject the neoliberal account of (hyper) rational judgements and autonomous actions as being somehow detached, neutral processes. Reason and rational judgement are not invulnerable processes but are subject to a range of obstacles such as indoctrination, misinformation, propaganda, deception, and so on. This does not mean that we cannot use our reasoning capacity to question our culture, information and history. Clearly we can. Relativism is, as Ernest Gellner remarked, the problem, not the solution, to our understanding of the natural and social world (Gellner, 1985). It does, however, suggest that reason is not invulnerable and is subject to a range of pressures and forces that limit it.

The concept of political culture is far from uncontested, but, following Schlesinger and Kevin (2000: 210), I define political culture as the institutions and procedures that help to structure a particular political order and the beliefs, meanings and values that people attach to them. In social theory this can be presented more abstractly as a concern with issues of structure and agency, for reasons that I will come to shortly. The neoliberal vision of the (hyper) rational individual is of someone pursuing his or her egoistic desires and wants in the marketplace as a consumer or in political life as a citizen. This abstract, egoistic rational individual is (ideally) independent of external influences in the process of making these rational choices. Whilst they can listen to and compare ideas, goods, and so on, the position of the neoliberal rational individual is summed up by a refrain that is often heard in daily life, *'no one tells me what to think.'* This powerful libertarian idea argues very strongly for a sense of human agency in which the individual makes up his or her own mind about issues *freely and in an uncoerced fashion.* This is a defence of the idea that in an open society where there are diverse forms of information available to us we can compare and contrast differing ideas before making up our minds as to which is the best for our particular wants and desires. Only in totalitarian societies can we say that the general populace are susceptible to media propaganda as the flows of information are directly controlled by the state. Thus the ideal mechanism for promoting human autonomy is a capitalist market-organised communications industry, as it will provide people with what they want by responding to their demands, rather than a state-led system which attempts to tell people what they need (Friedman, 1962). Capitalist communications markets promote diversity, openness and pluralism to the extent that people demand it.

This is a series of powerful and common claims but they are limited in their analyses of rationality, choices and social power and in order to explain why this is so we need to recognise their philosophical and empirical failings. Starting with the philosophical weaknesses, this model of human agency depends very much upon the idea that rational actors are in the position of the view from nowhere. By this I mean the idea that nothing *in particular* influences us when we make our rational judgements other than hard reason. We are the beings of Bentham's felecific calculus, continually weighing up what is in our egoistic interests. This liberal conception of the rational individual is flawed on a number of grounds, despite its ideological appeal, and I want to focus upon two here. First, it has no sense of historical context, by which I mean here the idea of a political culture. Second, it does not explain the way in which media markets and institutions work in practice, as opposed to in theory.

With regard to the question of political culture, we return again to the question of structure and agency. Many neoliberal writers have attacked critics of capitalism for presenting a strongly determinist (structural) account of human agency in order to explain why it is that people support a system that has such significant drawbacks. On this critical view, according to the neoliberal argument, people are presented as dupes, unable to make independent choices and always having choices imposed upon them in a manner of which they are unaware (Archer, 1995; Jensen, 1990; Thompson, 1990). Only the trained social theorist is apparently able to see through this in order to expose what is really taking place. Capitalist markets shape people's choices rather than respond to them. On a rhetorical level it is not hard to see why the neoliberal defence of human agency should have the appeal that it does. However, while the structuralist view of rational choices and human autonomy is indeed often overly deterministic, the neoliberal perspective is equally prone to being wildly voluntaristic, that is, hyper-rational. For the neoliberal it would appear that as Karl Popper once argued, '*anything is possible in human affairs*' (1962: 197). We can choose and do whatever we wish. This assumption is deeply problematic. Just as the extreme structuralist account suggests that we have no real choices, so the neoliberal view says that we have open-ended choices. Both are flawed and a sketch of the role that political culture plays in both constraining, motivating and enabling the rational choices we make in our lives will illustrate why this is so.

*Contra* the neoliberal view of rational, autonomous choices as the view from nowhere, a concern with political culture forces us to recognise that when we make rational judgements we are always doing so with a view from somewhere. We are born into social orders where there are prevailing institutions, social structures, habits, values, procedures and beliefs that are part of our upbringing. As has long been recognised by a range of writers, the mainstream media have and continue to play a crucial role in the construction of national identities and the socialisation of people into modern nation-states (Thompson, 1990; Smith, 1991; Schlesinger, 1991). The neoliberal view of hyper-rational autonomy as the view from nowhere is wrong for this very simple reason: our ideas, values, habits and beliefs are built in response to the social and historical conditions in which we find ourselves. Thus, at any given time what we take to be normal, good, bad, right, wrong, and so on, will *in part* be in response to prevailing norms, customs, institutions and procedures, and not because we have a divine access to pure reason or our rational ego. However, this emphasis upon political culture, the view from somewhere, should not be seen as a simple defence of a modified form of structuralism in which we have *no* choices. On the contrary, we *do* have the capacity to question the practices, values and beliefs that structure and permeate our ideas and our society. This, then, is the crucial point: in order to do so we need diverse, open and plural institutions available to us where we can exchange ideas, obtain alternate sources of information and engage in meaningful analyses of the existing social order. This is why the role of the communications industry is so important in our capacity to make rational, autonomous judgements, as it is the primary source of information about social, economic and political life for the majority of people. The media industries do not tell us what to think *per se,* but importantly for most of us they do tell us *what* issues and events to think about and *how* to think about them. The liberal analysis of capitalist media markets suggests that they are neutral mechanisms, purveyors of unadulterated information for society. In this sense they are the ultimate institutional defenders of the view from nowhere. However, this view from nowhere does not exist and this has important implications for questions of ownership and control of the media and the role that it plays in promoting or defending human autonomy. What interests do the owners and controllers of mainstream media institutions actually have as political and economic agents? What relationship do they have to existing political institutions? I have offered answers to these questions throughout the course of the book.

The extent to which we are able to make rational, autonomous judgements depends upon a great many things besides the nature of the dominant institutions in our political culture. It will also depend upon more mundane matters such as the time, money and energy we can put into seeking out and evaluating different accounts of events and issues, goods and services. There are severe structural constraints to our capacity to make rational choices that the neoliberal view of capitalist markets and perfect information seems to pay relatively little heed to. These constraints are reflected in the earlier concerns I have expressed over the idea of global citizenship that fails to pay sufficient heed to the problems of material inequality and poverty. The question that needs to be addressed is how did these institutions, practices, procedures, values and beliefs emerge historically? Whose interests do they reflect and which social groups have had the power to bring them into being and for what purposes?

A focus upon political culture means that, in part, we are concerned with questions of structure and agency within particular social orders. There are, of course, institutions, procedures and practices that are distinct to the British political culture, for example. None the less, as I mentioned at the beginning of this book, human security is a concern with global human security. It recognises the interrelated structure of the world order and that the rise of capitalism and the modern state-system has been a systemic or general trend that has shaped it. Thus our analysis is focused upon these general tendencies as well as the particular, concrete practices that shape the social and political orders that make up the modern world orders. A concern with particular political cultures is a concern with differences in the political institutions and structure of world order, it is not to treat political cultures as independent parts. Rather, following Wallerstein, they are distinct political parts of an integrated global economic and political system (Wallerstein, 1991). They are always to be viewed in the context of their relationship to these general tendencies. What we can see from this is that particular political cultures provide us with the frames of meaning and reference from which a common-sense understanding of political economy emerges. As Robert Cox has often argued, what constitutes common sense is never simply an expression of some neutrally discerned popular will but is always an expression of the power of those dominant social groups who have sought to use the means of communication to disseminate such understandings of the world (Cox, 1996) and which therefore sets potentially powerful obstacles to our autonomy and our ability to make rational judgements. We are never outside of our culture and history in our analyses, we are always looking from within it. Again, this does not mean that rationality and autonomy are meaningless concepts. On the contrary, *the idea of the public sphere is important precisely because it offers us the arena within which a genuinely rational and uncoerced consensus about social order might be derived.* We have the capacity for criticism and self-criticism of our society, beliefs and so on, if we choose to or have the means necessary to do so. Rationality and autonomy are important aspirations for providing legitimate grounds for a just social order, but they do not mean what the neoliberal model suggests.

*Ideology, Interests and Power – The Limits to Human Autonomy*
In many respects ideology is a distinctly unfashionable concept unless one means by it simply that everyone's view is ideological.[7] The problem with the latter view is that it obliterates the critical role that the concept has come to play in social and political analysis. For my purposes ideology has two main meanings: first, an ideology can be seen as a coherent set of beliefs and values held by a particular social group. In this sense the concept has an empirical, descriptive meaning. Second, ideology means, to paraphrase John Thompson, 'language or meaning in the service of power' (Thompson, 1990: 56). This definition can have a strong and a weak meaning. The strong version argues that the values, beliefs and ideas of subordinate groups in any given social order, are the product of the power of dominant groups to construct and impose them through a dominant culture/ideology. The weak version says that in any given epoch or particular social order, there will be a series of values, beliefs and ideas that tend to be dominant in shaping the policies and practices of the major political, economic and cultural institutions of the day. While these ideas, values and beliefs reflect the interests of powerful or dominant social groups, it does not mean that subordinate groups will necessarily accept them as being true, right, and so on. The first approach is an 'effects' claim in that it argues that the effect of the dominant ideology is to dupe subordinate groups in society into accepting their fate.[8] The second approach is primarily descriptive/explanatory and claims that there is or can be a dominant ideology that reflects the interests of elites. It is the second approach which I am advocating here as a necessary feature of any critical analysis of the communications industry. The global communications industry is thoroughly ideological in this sense: they are the purveyors of pro-capitalist, pro-private enterprise values. In this sense 'language in the service of power' means that the mainstream global media will tend to reflect the interests of the powerful elites that dominate the institutions that structure world order. As Herman and McChesney (1997) note, they generally support a pro-capitalist agenda that coincides with the neoliberal political economy model. The power exercised here is a power to frame, represent and select issues. As Herman and McChesney write, the owners and controllers of global communication tend to be overwhelmingly conservative capitalists – it should not be too surprising that their institutions tend to reflect this.[9]

Why then, do neoliberals not focus upon this issue in any depth? Neoliberals will argue that the market is simply providing people with what they want and this is what the framing, representation and selection of issues reflects. The media act as a mirror of society and its demands. This, however, is a weak argument as media markets are not simply open reflections of changing patterns of demand but are guided mechanisms whose production patterns are structured by the dominant capitalist institutions within them. Media markets are not 'free' in the sense that they are open to meaningful or widespread competition and nor is success in the media marketplace determined by sales. Profitability is a product of securing advertising revenue for broadcasters and newspapers alike. This leads to a perversion of so-called market principles where rather than the success or failure of a media commodity being determined by its popularity with consumers, it is determined by the ability of producers to sell an audience to advertisers (Bagdikian, 1992). As James Curran has shown, in Britain the collapse of a working-class press including the very popular *Daily Herald* is everything to do with the increasing costs of production and distribution in the print industry, something that has ultimately led the print media to dependence upon advertising revenue (Curran, 1991). Rather than the Fourth Estate of privately run and owned media being independent of both state and commercial pressures, they are utterly dependent upon states and capitalist businesses for revenue, sources, legitimacy, licensing, protection of property rights, and so on (McManus, 1994; Garnham, 1990). In addition, neoliberal ideology is not simply a coherent set of values, beliefs and ideas about the world. It is also an ideology in the critical sense that I set out above – that is, it reflects the interests of the powerful political, economic and cultural elites that dominate the institutions and processes that structure world order. It is understandably important for neoliberals to attack the idea of ideology as critique as being an elitist concept that presents sections of the population as misguided at best, idiots at worst. However, this is not what is implied by the approach to ideology as critique that I have set out here. On the contrary, how people respond to the dominant values, beliefs and ideas passed on through the various social and cultural institutions that shape any given social order will reflect a variety of complex factors. There is nothing predetermined or straightforward about the effects of a dominant ideology upon people in general. We possess the capacity for intellectual self-defence but it invariably hinges upon our ability to find resources with which to challenge established views. The importance of the neoliberal ideology is that it is an attempt to legitimise the existing structure of social power in world order: the power of global elites. Its success or failure over time and space will depend upon the extent to which subordinate groups have the means of challenging these received ideas and practices. *Hence, ownership and control of the means of communication is a vital issue for human autonomy and security precisely because it is the means of communication that lies at the heart of the possibility of meaningful political analysis, discussion and criticism of existing institutions and ways of doing things.*

Thus, ideology is relevant to us precisely because it suggests that there are limits to rationality and autonomy that are both institutional and ideational. If the means of communication are increasingly privately owned and commodified, then public service principles are forced to transform themselves to become more commercially viable; power is shifting into the hands of private institutions and interests and out of the hands of democratically accountable bodies. This is not to overstate the democratic credentials of public service broadcasters but there is, none the less, an important point of principle here about the role that the means of communication plays in any given social order.[10] The question that arises is: are the means of communication simply another industry or do they raise particular political, economic and ethical issues that demand that they be controlled in the public interest rather than private interest? My argument is that shifting ownership and control of the means of communication increasingly into private hands is deeply problematic for democracy, in the same way that state control of the means of communication is an obstacle to the possibility of any kind of democracy in authoritarian countries. In effect, power and control over the flow of ideas are shifted into the hands of private elites whose interests are profit and the maintenance of their own position and power in society. *It reinforces the tyranny of the minority at the expense of the public good.* As a consequence, the public sphere is further eroded and becomes a realm structured and controlled by the interests of private power. What we are increasingly moving towards is a global corporate ideology, propagated in part by the global communications industries, which aspire to controlling political, economic and cultural life *in toto.* Democracy and autonomy are problematic for these private tyrannies precisely because they might render the control of resources and institutions, the things needed to satisfy human needs and autonomy, under popular control. Clearly this would go directly against the grain of the values, beliefs and ideas of neoliberal ideology that wants in practice to defend the idea that private tyrannies should own and control ever more of the institutions and resources that structure our lives. In this sense, neoliberalism is fundamentally anti-democratic and anti-human security, and pro-private tyranny.

It is unsurprising, then, that when we look at the political cultures of the core capitalist states such as Britain and the US we find that political campaigning and advertising is not based upon promoting rational choices but appeals to other factors such as emotion, fear and prejudice. As Kathleen Hall Jamieson notes in *Dirty Politics*, for example, fear and nostalgia are prevailing themes of political advertising in the US and Britain and this is no surprise. If you want to control people, fear is a potent mechanism for doing so. As Jamieson notes, fear of immigrants, crime, welfare scroungers, foreigners in general, are all pervasive themes in US and British political life (Jamieson, 1992). While it is the case that political campaigning has always been able to use such tactics, what is qualitatively different in the late twentieth and early twenty-first centuries is that with the rise of new forms of communication and of mass democratic societies, propaganda has taken on new levels and ever more resources (Jackall, 1995; Carey, 1997). In this respect, one of the defining features of the twentieth century was not only the spread of political propaganda but also of corporate propaganda under the guidance of the public relations industry. While political propaganda is well documented and normalised as a part of political processes, corporate propaganda is comparatively underexamined. As Elizabeth Fones-Wolf, among others, has noted, corporations have long had an interest in trying to shape the 'public mind', in Lippmann's words (Fones-Wolf, 1994). This has taken a variety of bewildering forms, from advertising and marketing through to the funding of political parties, indoctrination programmes for workers under the guise of 'educational programs', think tanks and policy institutes, trade unions and charities. This can all quite reasonably be seen as an attempt on the part of corporate interests to influence both the political agenda and in practice to attack the critical autonomy of ordinary citizens (Gill, 1995; Van Der Pijl, 1998).

In the neoliberal version of the information society, ideology is absent and power is seen as being largely relocated back into the hands of ordinary citizens and away from states and corporations alike. In reality, the information society is a complex process of transformation in world order which intensifies state and corporate power while also having the potential for citizens and subordinate social groups to attempt to alter social life for the good. A primary role of the global communications industries is to promote the neoliberal ideology that seeks to legitimise the developments in private corporate power and the restructured role of the state as an inevitable and natural outcome of capitalist markets. This is a new 'common sense' that cuts across the political divide in governing circles. There is, then, a form of 'global governance' that has emerged in the past twenty-five years and it is premised on the principles of the global corporate ideology I have mentioned here. Simply expressed, its main rhetorical premise is that private power is good and that the public sector is not to be trusted. The tools of disseminating this ideology are nothing to do with encouraging rational choices *per se*, but rest upon the power to intimidate and scare electorates through such familiar tactics as the 'problems' said to be caused by immigrants, the unemployed, foreigners, change in general, and so on (Golding and Middleton, 1982). Invariably we find that these political scapegoats tend to be those with the least power, influence or authority in society, in effect, those that are easiest to victimise. The private institutions that have the real power to shape and control the lives of citizens, consumers and workers alike are very rarely the focus of political campaigning or media attack, for reasons that should be palpably clear. The global public sphere has been increasingly hollowed out as a realm of substantive and critical debate about public and private institutions. Where then, does this leave us with our concern for human security and the public sphere?

## Conclusions: Human Security and the Public Sphere in an Age of Information

> The public sphere is a realm of our social life in which something approaching public opinion can be formed with access guaranteed to all citizens. (Habermas, 1974: 49)

There are a number of principles that are said to underpin the public sphere in Habermas's account and three are of particular significance to our concern with human security and autonomy: first, the idea that there should be a general accessibility to the public sphere for all citizens; second, the removal of privileged access to any particular group, individual or institution, and finally the idea that in so doing uncoerced communication will enable us to discover rational and consensually agreed norms of social order. Of these three principles, the last is an ideal to be strived for while the first two are prerequisites for the idea of the good society. A social order riven by social inequalities of class, gender, race, and so on, is not one in which human security can be established for all or to any lasting degree. As will hopefully be clear by now hierarchy and inequality in a capitalist world order renders the idea of equal access to the public sphere deeply flawed in practice. Major corporate and political actors have privileged access to the various public spheres (at local, national, regional and global levels) through which they are able to set out and defend the ideology that promotes their own power, interests and authority.

For some neoliberals, the implications of the information society are that they are potentially reinventing the public sphere and enhancing the power of citizens on a number of levels. The reality of this, as we have seen, is far more problematic. At best the potential is there for citizens to act at the four levels of world order. In practice, in order to understand these developments and the policy changes that have embedded them we must consider who has introduced these changes in NIT and why. Overwhelmingly what we find is that NIT has been introduced by states and transnational corporations (TNCs) with a view to enhancing either a state's military power or surveillance and control of domestic populations, or alternately it has been introduced by corporations with a view to disciplining workforces and enhancing profit. Only contingently is there a connection to the satisfaction of human needs and human autonomy. The private control of information and knowledge through the privatisation of communications is a global trend that has seen the uneven retreat of public service broadcasting directed at the satisfaction of public communication needs. In terms of power and knowledge, the private control of information and the enhanced monitoring power of states surely erodes the autonomy and freedom of citizens as part of an ongoing global tendency. In the concluding chapter to this book, I want to look at what these tendencies mean in terms of the idea of communication needs as we move towards a global public sphere and how the means of communication might be organised in order to promote human security.

## CHAPTER 6

# Global Communication, Human Security and the Challenge to the Public Sphere

## *Globalisation and Human Security*

What has been presented here is the way in which neoliberal political economy acts as an ideology that serves to justify and explain the changes taking place in world order in general and global communication in particular. In practice, there are fundamental differences between the neoliberal rhetorical commitment to such concepts as 'free trade' and individual liberty and the practices of core capitalist states and corporations. This has led to a system that I have termed 'corporate mercantile capitalism'. The global communications companies that are the central concern of this book have been at the forefront of pressing for these changes through the available state mechanisms, nationally, regionally and globally. The symbiotic relationship between the corporations and state and governing institutions of the core capitalist states has led to a situation in which policy processes are increasingly subject to the control and influence of private power. This has led in turn to the principle of public subsidy for private power becoming embedded in global political economy. As has been argued, this has disastrous consequences for human security and human autonomy, increasingly taking control, ownership and decision making out of the hands of public and democratic institutions and into the hands of private tyrannies, pursuing their own ends of profit and expanding their commercial empires. The analogy with an economic war is appropriate here as largely G7-based communications corporations seek to carve up the global economy in their own interests (Herman and McChesney, 1997). These trends link into wider processes of globalisation, tendencies that are being driven by a range of structures and mechanisms that I focused upon earlier in this book. As with any social system these are not predetermined processes with inevitable outcomes. On the contrary, we are dealing with open systems within which a range of tendencies, mechanisms and actors are able to exert influence and pressure upon events. I want to focus here upon globalisation itself and the role that global communications companies play in this process and what, in turn, this tells us about human security. There are two major strands to globalisation that I want to focus upon, which I have termed globalisation from above (GFA) and globalisation from below (GFB).

## Globalisation From Above (GFA)

As has been made clear throughout this book, the issue of human security cannot be understood without situating it in the context of political economy in general. The political-economic institutions, structures and processes that enable and constrain social relations at the four levels of world order are central to any critical analysis of world order that is concerned with the possible attainment of human security. The role of the global communications industry in shaping ongoing tendencies in the global economy and the restructuring of inter-state relations has been pivotal on two particular counts.

### Infrastructure and Ideas

First, the communications industries have provided infrastructure in the form of software and hardware that has enabled corporations in general to alter their patterns of production, invariably enhancing the power of corporations at the expense of workforces. Second, the global communications corporations themselves are the major purveyors of news, information, entertainment and knowledge about the world in general. The power of ideas is a crucial factor for the possibility of progressive social change and the communications corporations are the prime purveyors of ideas in the world today. If they are not open to diverse forms of social, political and economic criticism, then they act to narrow the range of ideas in popular discourse.

In infrastructural terms it is reasonably clear that the prime movers towards a global economy (marked by a complex array of policies of liberalisation, protectionism, deregulation and privatisation) have been the core capitalist states and their companies. It is these who have had the power to construct and impose (where necessary) the rules and regulations of global political economy. The last General Agreement on Tariffs and Trade (GATT) Round is a classic example of this form of global power as rules were changed to liberalise global trade in areas where the US and other Western countries have tremendous advantages. Good examples of this are the so-called trade-related intellectual property rights (TRIPs) and trade-related investment measures (TRIMs). The liberalisation of these markets has enabled rich Western corporations to privatise such things as agricultural seeds. The fact that these seeds were the products of the work of generations of farmers, often in the Third World (periphery), working and pooling their knowledge and resources in such a manner that the idea of sole patent or copyright is impossible to determine, is irrelevant. Seeds and other goods are now 'owned' by Western agri-business and farmers in the developing world no longer have the right to reuse seeds on a yearly basis or to simply give them away to neighbours, friends, and so on, without breaking these TRIPs (*Third World Resurgence*, 1995). In other areas where competition might be unduly harmful to the economies of these core capitalist states (areas such as textiles, agriculture and clothing), the movement towards freer trade has to be controlled and managed so as to minimise the threat to their economic interests, what E.H. Carr once described as 'Free Trade imperialism' (Watkins, 1999; Carr, 1995: 47–8). In practice, the volumes of market theory that litter the libraries of the world's universities have limited relevance to the real world of political economic relations. As writers such as Henwood and Kanth have shown, the abstract mathematical models on which the assumptions of neoliberal political economy are based are so divorced from the actual workings of real markets that their main deductive assumptions about how markets work in practice are not simply problematic, they are wrong. Actually existing capitalism is a very different form of social relation from the abstract pictures presented in the theoretical tomes of neoliberal political economy. It is closer to being a war between corporate empires than it is to ideal competition.

What we can see, then, is that global communication provides the infrastructural technology that has enabled capitalist companies in general to take advantage of and indeed to push, lobby, cajole, bribe and coerce, where necessary, governments into legitimising the changes in global political economy that I have discussed earlier.[1] In related fashion, states have been key actors in bringing about these globalising tendencies as I set out in Chapter 2, and they too have benefited from the hardware and software of the global communications industries. Again, though, we need to be nuanced in our analysis here. Not all states have benefited from these changes and not all have benefited in the same way. Core capitalist states have been able to use the infrastructure to coordinate a range of political and military activities, from planning and practising wars through to the control and surveillance of populations for threats to state security. In Europe, for example, the sharing of information between nationally based police forces and the movement towards European-wide policing would be impossible without the communications infrastructure needed to organise such activity (Statewatch, 2000). The threat to human security and autonomy from these tendencies is stark, as both states and companies alike build up huge databases of information on citizens, pushing back the boundary between public and private realms to dangerous degrees. In global terms, the use of the hardware and software of global communication companies is recognised as an important form of power in geopolitics. The control of information and the use of technology to fight wars, gather information and to carry out continual surveillance of the world's states and the communication transactions of individual citizens is now firmly in the hands of the world's core capitalist states, most importantly and powerfully, the US (Nye and Owens, 1992). Far from eroding the so-called sovereignty and autonomy of states in general, globalisation has dramatically enhanced the power of the core capitalist states to police and structure the world as they see fit. The alliance between corporate and geopolitical interests that shapes global political economy reflects the interrelated interests of these governing elites. The institutions, structures and procedures that they promote stand as major obstacles to the goals of human security.

With regard to the power of ideas, as Herman and McChesney have powerfully argued, the global communications industry has steadily moved towards more commercial forms of ownership and control (Herman and McChesney, 1997). In their relentless pursuit of mergers as a means to dominate markets and generate higher profits they generally tend to promote an ideology of 'corporate capitalism'. By this they mean a general tendency to support capitalism and private power against its potential critics. Empirically, this is a claim about the forms of mainstream communication and information in the core capitalist states, but one that is also true of the world's media in general. They are increasingly privately owned and ultimately tend to present a constrained range of debate about the legitimacy of established capitalist and political institutions. For example, in Britain prior to the last election, the Labour Party assiduously sought the support of what had been, with a few exceptions, a largely hostile national press. What this suggests is perhaps unproblematic, that major corporations will tend to support whichever political party promotes policies that would appear to be in their best interests. While there are no doubt other factors to be considered, this seems to be an unobjectionable assumption, one confirmed, in fact, by Rupert Murdoch in an interview with the BBC's 'The Money Programme' (Murdoch, 1995). The problem with this, of course, is that democracies are not meant to be run by and in the interests of powerful private organisations (tyrannies, if we are to be accurate as to their structural make-up), but are about the participation of and responsiveness to the needs of the general public. The development of GFA has enhanced the power of global companies in general to exert ever more influence, power and control over policy making at all four levels of world order, largely at the expense of effective democratic control.

The idea of global civil society that has been at the heart of GFA and neoliberal ideology is revealed in practice as substantially shaped by the powerful political-economic institutions and actors who have created it. For the neoliberal, civil and global civil society represents the extension of human freedom and possibility, the realm of risks and the entrepreneur (Cavallo, 1999). In practice it tends to serve as an extension of the realm of freedom and power for those that already have it; the political, economic and cultural institutions of the core capitalist states have forced through these changes to global political economy of the past three decades. Often this has been with the help of willing elites in the developing world, sometimes against them. In general though, this has been carried out at the expense of the interests of working and non-working people, undermining the institutions upon which their lives tend to be built: public education, health, housing, transport, and so on (Merrien, 1998; Chomsky, 1994: Part 2). For those states and peoples unwilling to fall in line with the 'Washington Consensus'[2] with regard to adopting the correct mix of policies of liberalisation, privatisation, protectionism and deregulation, there are a number of sanctions on offer through either the World Trade Organization (WTO) or unilaterally imposed by the US. The US's peculiar trade legislation 'Super 301' enables it to unilaterally impose sanctions against those states that threaten the hegemony of its political and corporate elites and their interests. Walden Bello notes how such tactics have been used against Brazil, India, Thailand, Taiwan and Singapore. The case of Thailand was particularly revealing: in the late 1980s, the Thai government, acting out of concerns over public health, wanted to limit the sale of high-tar tobacco brands. This proved to be unacceptable to US business and political elites who used Super 301 to punish Thailand until it conformed to the 'international norm' (Bello et al., 1993: 80–82). As President Wilson once said, the United States had been 'founded for the benefit of humanity' (Carr, 1995: 73). A happy coincidence! This example illustrates the kind of structural, institutional and procedural obstacles that confront those arguing for or working towards human security. Global civil society, built and shaped by the impact of new information technology (NIT), has served to enhance the power of political, economic and cultural institutions and elites, to shape and direct policy making at all levels of world order.

## World Orders and Historical Structures

David Harvey has noted that the history of capitalism is in part the history of the means of communication (Harvey, 1973: 149). The same might easily be argued for the history of states and political institutions. The means of communication have been the pivotal infrastructural technology and institutional forces in the rise of the modern world order since the sixteenth century. This has generally been shaped by the structures, institutions and procedures of global capitalism and the inter-state system. These twin structures of world order have, in turn, largely been dominated by the political and economic elites who in the course of the twentieth century came to establish transnational links to coordinate their interests wherever possible as opposed to allowing conflicts to break out into global warfare.

To say that there are structures to world order means simply that the social relations of everyday life that connect local, national, regional and global levels of world order are not simply unconstrained and contingent events. Rather, it is to recognise that there are necessary constraints as well as contingent possibilities to everyday life and that the nature of these constraints is taking increasingly complex and interconnected forms. The institutions and procedures that constrain, motivate and enable how people live are increasingly interlocked at the four main levels of world order. The idea that world order is only composed of national economies or discrete nation-states is to simplify and ultimately mask the reality of social relations that are far more complex. Any attempt to explain the current obstacles to human security, which fails to recognise the integrated nature of this global system, will be flawed. It will fail to locate the causal mechanisms and structures that underpin existing social relations, resting as they do upon the complex interplay of necessary conditions established by global capitalism and the geopolitics of the inter-state system. This must always be seen in conjunction with the contingent factors of particular institutions, populations and procedures at specific times and places. For example, in practical terms this translates quite simply as recognising that within Britain the existing mainstream media institutions are subject to the pressures of both global capitalism (the need to find profits) and geopolitics (the regulation of activities by nation-states). At the same time, Britain's media institutions are also subject to the contingent factors of the country as a nation-state, its particular forms of political, economic and cultural institutions and procedures. In addition to this, and crucially, British media companies are also agents themselves: they can and do act to try and change the conditions of the institutions, structures and practices in which they find themselves, be they at a local, national, regional or a global level. Thus, in Britain, the major media corporations have sought to encourage elected governments to expand the commercial sector of broadcasting and to relax the rules and regulation of cross-media ownership (Negrine, 1996: Chapter 10). Whilst this is undoubtedly a global trend, it is also subject to the particular conditions of British political culture with its strong history of public service broadcasting. As such, the outcome of such a struggle is not predetermined. What happens in Britain will be subject to a range of institutions and agents with often countervailing interests, and we should not expect to see exactly the same outcomes as we see in France, Brazil or the US (Hay, 2000).[3] There may be a general tendency in global political economy towards privatisation, for example, but privatisation can and does take a number of different forms, which will reflect the concrete circumstances, and history of particular political systems (*Journal of International Affairs*, 1997).

Thus to talk of historical structures is to be concerned with the development of world order and the agents and institutions that have brought it into being. It is to recognise that while there are structures to world order, these are often complex and will only partially endure. The institutions and the structures that are generated can and do change over time. They have been made by people and they can be altered or transformed accordingly. This is a crucial point for human security as it is to argue that people are not *necessarily* forced to accept that the currently existing world order with its structures, procedures and institutions is the best that can be achieved. However, in order to move towards global human security it requires the spread of both ideas and action on the part of a range of actors in world order and for this reason it is necessary now to turn to the alternate tendency of globalisation, that which I have termed globalisation from below (GFB).

## Globalisation From Below (GFB)

The history of world order is not simply the expression of the power of succeeding generations of elites to build the structures, institutions and procedures that constrain, motivate and enable our lives. As writers such as Barrington Moore, Theda Skocpol and Immanuel Wallerstein have made clear in their historical sociological studies, it is primarily the conflict between elite or ruling classes *and* subordinate social groups that have structured the development of world order. It is these struggles that have led to the range of political, economic and cultural institutions, structures and procedures that make up world order. While world order is structured by the general tendencies of global capitalism and the geopolitics of the inter-state system, these tendencies manifest themselves in different political, economic and cultural forms in different times and places. It is this complex interplay between necessary and contingent factors that provides the broad macro-historical understanding of the emergence of the modern world order. Concrete analysis tries to relate the particular events, institutions, agents and procedures within, and in relation to, these broader structures. Thus, changes in the patterns of ownership and control of the British media industry need to be understood in relation to the particular institutions, agents and practices of British political culture and its relationship to the wider structuring forces of global capitalism and geopolitical interests.

Globalisation appears to be making these interrelations of structures and agents more complex and dynamic than ever but it does so in part because globalisation is still a process of struggle between social groups over the resources that shape our lives. Thus GFB is the part played by subordinate social groups in the ongoing process of globalisation, mirroring Polanyi's idea of a double-movement in which social groups seek to regulate and control markets in order to protect themselves from their socially destructive potentials. We can see this in a way that mirrors GFA.

*Infrastructure and Ideas*

The infrastructural changes that NIT and the world's global communications companies have brought to world order are not simply the preserve of powerful political, military, economic and cultural institutions. On the contrary, it is clear that a range of sub-state and non-state actors operating on an international scale have sought to use NIT for a range of political, economic and cultural reasons. Beyer has noted the ways in which many religious institutions are seeking to extend and revive their potential audiences through coordinated and world-wide practices, utilising the means of communication to disseminate their ideas (Beyer, 1994). Equally, we can point to myriad institutions from trade unions, human rights groups and environmental groups through to think-tanks and fascist movements who have all sought both to spread their ideas and to organise their activities on scales that increasingly transcend the nation-state. Recent examples include the world-wide protests against the last GATT Round and the recent protests against the major institutions of global capitalism such as the WTO (Wilkin, 2000). GFB is the realm of civil society where struggle over the political, economic and cultural institutions, structures and procedures that shape world order is most directly played out by the world's citizenry. It is the realm where the movements concerned with the end-goals of human security (the satisfaction of human needs and autonomy) are most active.

None the less, this realm of global civil society remains substantively shaped by the institutions that have led GFA, in terms of the control of the means of communication, the means of production and the means of violence. There is a clear hierarchy of power here and it would simply be false or naive to view global civil society as a realm of equal actors. Even within GFB there are many agents, perhaps the most important, who represent the interests of those institutions and elites who shape GFA. Think-tanks, NGOs such as the National Endowment for Democracy (NED) and a variety of religious groups (though clearly not all), can be seen as part of a wider coalition of forces promoting ideas and practices supportive of the institutions that already structure world order (Gill, 1990; Van Der Pijl, 1998). As a consequence, they are part of the extension of elite power that helps to shape world order and which stands as an obstacle to human security. However, it is important to recognise that GFB represents a fluid and growing realm of activity and communication that has many (and potential) allies for human security. For example, writers such as Jeremy Brecher have focused upon the disparate range of non-state actors organising globally around workers' rights, human rights, environmental and gender issues, who have the potential to present and push for a progressive political agenda that is global rather than simply local or national (Brecher et al., 1993). The importance of global civil society is that it is a realm within which such groups can communicate and coordinate their activities. Its weakness is that the interests and institutional structures that have brought it into being are tied primarily to elite interests rather than general human needs. The possibility of human security rests upon the extent to which such institutions and elite actors can be transformed and challenged. In concluding this book I want to return to the idea of the global public sphere and human security to reassert why the former is so important for the latter.

## The Global Public Sphere and Human Security

The general theme of this book has been a concern with the role that autonomy plays as part of human security. In particular I have sought to examine the way in which tendencies in global communication have led and are continuing to lead towards the increased commercialisation of the industry and the commodification of communication and information. The logic of this has been to enhance private power at the expense of the public good, promoting an ethos of 'corporate mercantile capitalism' to help justify and explain the necessity for the wider changes in global political economy. Habermas's conclusion was that the public sphere had been 'refeudalised' by developments in the means of communication, rendered subordinate to the interests of powerful private institutions in conjunction with state elites. While there is much to support this argument it is also to overlook the possibilities that the NIT revolution in global communication brings to the public sphere. Public spheres are no longer simply local or national realms of political debate and analysis; they are now, more firmly than ever, also regional and global in their reach. Popular outcry in the core capitalist countries against famine, hunger or injustice cannot easily be dismissed by their respective governments, although they might well attempt to manipulate them. Alex De Waal and Rakiya Omaar show how this happened, for example, in the case of Ethiopia in the mid-1980s and the same argument can be made for both interventions in Somalia and Haiti in the 1990s, not to mention countless other interventions and non-interventions alike (De Waal and Omar, 1994). The fact that governing elites feel the need to do this is not in itself insignificant. As Chomsky and Herman have noted in their work on media propaganda, it would be a lot easier to tell the truth to the general public than it is to lie about events. The fact that governing elites feel the need to do this suggests that they are far from confident that the general populace would be happy to go along with the real reasons for such interventions, bound up as they are with issues of national geopolitical interest and business interests.

It is here that the problem of autonomy and human security is most acute. Given that, for most working and non-working people, the broadcast media are the prime source of information about the world, it is crucial that a diverse, plural, open and critical global media is able to present the information needed to make the global public sphere a place of real debate and activity. In reality, as has been shown throughout this book, the world's mainstream media institutions are narrowing in terms of ownership and control and becoming integrated with other capitalist industries. Thus the ownership and control of information is largely placed into fewer hands, working under a range of constraints such as the limitations of time and space for analysis of issues, the ideological requirements of capitalist institutions, while also remaining subject to the pressure of diverse political institutions and elites. Thus the driving tendency in global communication is towards growing commercialisation at the expense of public service broadcasting. As I have said throughout, this is not a blanket defence of public service broadcasting or a publicly funded print media as it has existed or does now, but it is a defence of the idea that the means of communication is a dangerous weapon to be placed in the hands of private institutions driven by profit interests as much as it is when placed in the hands of monopoly state power. The provision of information and the control of the means of communication are intrinsic to the possibility of a democratic society and human autonomy and as such are a public service, not mere commodities to be bought and sold. The further the structure of the ownership and control of the means of communication moves into the hands of private interests, the more severely the idea of information and communication as a public service is undermined. It is difficult to see how a global public sphere, which encourages and promotes autonomy can be reconciled with the interests of such unbridled private power.

The idea of communication needs rests upon the assumption that for a democratic society to function it must be one that promotes debate and analysis of issues which may not be popular in terms of audience figures but which are none the less important for scrutinising the institutions that govern us (Eyre, 1999). It is difficult to conceive of meaningful democracy where the means of communication are so heavily skewed in favour of the private institutions that are increasingly taking control of them. Given that these private institutions have their own political and economic interests that, understandably, they pursue as aggressively as possible, there is a clear dividing line for human security here. A commercially driven media tends to promote private interests that are in direct conflict with the communication needs of populations at large. To this end, some kind of public service broadcasting model(s) is appropriate for the goals of human security and autonomy.

However, the idea of civil society at local, national, regional or global levels of world order does not simply rest upon the ownership and control of the major means of communication. It is also a result of the activities of those engaged in civil society, at whichever level they are acting. Arrighi, Hopkins and Wallerstein (1989) have referred to these as anti-systemic groups, those concerned with challenging the forms of hierarchy and oppression upon which the current world order is partly based. These are undoubtedly important tendencies in world order and provide a crucial challenge to the orthodoxies of the mainstream global public sphere. Although this group is far from being homogeneous and is often contradictory in its aims, the agents most likely to promote human security are those groups working around such issues as workers' rights, feminism, the environment and human rights. The possibility of human security rests upon the extent to which these diverse groups can promote common interests and alternate forms of communication and debate against the institutions, structures, procedures and agents that are its primary obstacles. The twin systemic forces of world order – geopolitics and global capitalism – are both underpinned by ordering principles that are at the very least in conflict with the goals of human security. The political elites governing the inter-state system promote the idea of the national interest as the rational, guiding aim of policy. In practice, the national interest, as we have seen, is invariably the interest of the dominant political and economic elites, rather than the population as a whole. Global capitalism is driven by companies pursuing profit and is not geared towards the satisfaction of human needs or autonomy. The structures, institutions and procedures that make up these twin systems of world order present the major obstacles to the possibility of human security.

# Notes

## Introduction

1. A common theme in realist and neo-realist approaches to international relations that dominate the academic discipline in Anglo-American circles. For a recent overview see Dunne (1997). For a profound critique see Griffiths (1992).
2. In which Waltz (p. 9) quotes Erich Neede who comments how during the Cold War 'national security decision-making in some ... democracies (most notably in Western Germany) is actually penetrated by the US.'

## Chapter 1

1. William Bain (1999, 85) notes that 'the ethic of human security challenges and possibly undermines the moral foundation of international society as it has existed for nearly four-hundred years. Exponents of human security reject the sovereign state as the paramount moral community of international society; they do not believe that these communities ought to be the principle referents of security. Rather, the ethic of human security accords moral priority to the security of individual human beings.'
2. These should be seen as distinct levels of global order, related to each other but not reducible to each other in terms of effects, in the same way that structures and agents can be seen as being mutually constitutive but not simply reducible to each other. For an elaborate discussion of this, see Archer (1995: Chapter 3).
3. The appeal of behavioural social science in the US has been critically analysed by Peter T. Manicas (1987) who concludes that its attractions to capitalism and the state in terms of policy formation are important features in its intellectual legitimacy. Simply put, behaviourism is a defiantly uncritical analysis of society that eschews any normative concerns in its analysis on the assumption that such matters are unscientific and therefore beyond the pale of rational debate. Manicas's argument was foreshadowed in Chomsky's (1987) devastating attacks on the behaviourist psychology of B.F. Skinner.
4. Waltz is confusing on this point. In places he argues that the system cannot be independent of the unit (Keohane, 1986: 338). As a consequence Waltz says that neither system nor unit are determining. However, in his *Theory of International Politics* (1979: 69), a much stronger sense of structural (systemic) control is posited: 'The structure of a system acts as a constraining and disposing force, and because it does so systems theories explain and predict continuity within a

system.' The problem he faces given his assumptions about scientific model building is that in order for him to generate an explanatorily powerful theory from a few simple premises he must exclude a wide range of variables as they render quantification and calculation impossible. However, in so doing he is presenting us with what Sayer (1989) has called a violently abstract model that bears no relation to reality and therefore tells us nothing of practical use about international politics. Thus, the more factors that Waltz allows and the more he concedes to system-unit interaction the more his theory fails to adhere to its own positivist ambitions and deductive principles.

5. As Margaret Archer has argued, structures and agents may be co-determining but they are not simply the same thing: analytical dualism is needed to draw out the structural properties that provide a background within which and against which action takes place (Archer, 1995).

6. Waltz persists in his view that theories of international politics have some meaningful parallel with theories in physics, such as the study of the solar system, in a recent interview with F. Halliday and J. Rosenberg (1988: 383–4). In practice he seems oblivious to the pitfalls that such an approach presents to any explanation of international politics. On explanation in social science see Collier (1994: Chapter 6).

7. I would have liked to argue that I have the latent power to score a hat-trick for Arsenal but this would be to confuse latent powers with idealism, as was made clear to me by Cathal Smyth.

8. Within the most influential of the world's business press, the task now faced is not simply to downplay levels of poverty around the world but to deny that it exists at all. This philosophical idealism is part of the neoliberal approach to political economy with its idealised models of capitalism that according to Kanth (1999) have no bearing on the realities of actually existing capitalism. This idealism frequently leads neoliberal commentators and institutions to the conclusion that when reality fails to conform to these abstract models the problem lies not with the unreality of the models themselves, but with the failures of the general populace to make the necessary rational choices. This kind of infallible theory can lead writers such as Peter Huber (1999) in *Forbes* magazine to assert that *'The problem of poverty has been solved ... humanity finally triumphed over material scarcity, in America, at the close of the second millennium'*, a claim that sits rather uneasily alongside the US government's own report issued in 1999 which stated that 34 million Americans live in poverty (Apple Jnr, 2000; Kettle, 2000). Of course, one way around this is to redefine poverty until no one counts as being officially poor, a trick that governments around the world have utilised on countless occasions.

9. These are long-running themes in Wallerstein's work and have distanced him from orthodox Marxist critics who have tended to view capitalism as a necessary and ultimately progressive stage in human history.

10. Democratisation is defined in this sense to conform with the prescriptions of neoliberal global governance, which, as I will show later in the book, is a commitment to formal rather than substantive democratic procedures, with power over decision making and policy formation

increasingly dictated by private interests rather than public. That this has become an orthodoxy that cuts across the political spectrum is illustrated by a number of policy statements and speeches made by the Labour government in Britain which, despite its socialist history, embraces these principles in a seemingly uncritical manner. Thus Keith Vaz (2000) acting as FCO Minister of State could address an audience concerned with the Caspian region and say that 'the experience of some countries in South-East Asia has demonstrated that it is difficult, if not impossible, to achieve sustainable economic development in the absence of participatory democracy and respect for human rights and the rule of law. So it is very much in the long-term interests of the countries of the Caspian region to make progress in this area. And we and our EU partners are ready to support them in every way we can, because it is in our shared interest to do so.' Similar sentiments can be found in speeches by many European and North American politicians.

11. Lippmann wrote that 'Public opinion of the masses can't be counted upon to apprehend the reality of things with any speed' (1955: 26).

12. Sayer (2000: 19) notes the conceptual problems in conventional economic definitions of the service sector.

13. Rodrik (1997: 20) describes this: 'the ideological assault against the welfare state has made many governments unable to respond to the domestic needs of a more integrated economy.'

14. Clearly this is a complex issue. The selective interpretation of and response to human rights abuses is a major strand of debate in international relations literature.

## Chapter 2

1. A number of books explore this theme. For accounts of global communication see Comor (1994), Mowlana (1996); Frederick (1992), McChesney (1999).

2. It is the volume and speed of communications infrastructure that is at the heart of these qualitative shifts in the capacity of capitalism to reorganise itself across social time and space, bringing with it important changes in the organisation of social relations, work patterns, and so on. For contrasting accounts of this see Poster (1995), McChesney (1999), Castells (1996 and 1998), Sivanandan (1990).

3. See *The Guardian*, Media section, 24 July 1995 for a map setting out the reach of News Corporation.

4. This edited volume, for example, explores the long-term global aspirations of the major media news agencies.

5. There are important and wide-ranging debates here about the ontology of the world order and I do not wish to go into them in too great a depth as there is not sufficient space to do so. Suffice to say that I am broadly in agreement with Margaret Archer's account of an emergent social ontology that sees the world in terms of related but not reducible layers of reality, all of which combine to produce the complex and open structure of the world order at any given time. These layers can be seen as biological, psychological, cultural, social

and systemic properties. See Archer (1995) for a brilliant account of these ontological debates.

6.  The gini coefficient measures the extent to which the distribution of income (or, in some cases, consumption expenditures) among individuals or households within an economy deviates from a perfectly equal distribution. The coefficient ranges from Ø – meaning perfect equality – to 1 – complete inequality (UNDP, 1999: 254).

7.  For recent comment on the ways in which these pressure are being felt by sections of the US workforce, see Conlin (1999). On global poverty and inequality, see Shalom (1999), and *The Economist* (2000a).

8.  To clarify, the core capitalist states are those that have been central to the construction of the modern world order. It refers to those states that have built the institutional framework and established and enforce the rules (formal and informal) that bind the current world order. Thus it refers to the G7 states and primarily the United States which has been the hegemon underpinning world order for the past hundred years. This has been achieved either by force or by manufacturing a consent among a significant strata of the world's political and economic elites (Wallerstein, 1991).

9.  The liberalisation of the world economy needs to be understood in the context of the skewed nature of these processes of liberalisation that have evolved in recent decades, primarily through the GATT framework. As is often noted, this liberalisation does not equate with a classic 'free market' model of economic organisation. On the contrary, the liberalisation of trade has been both skewed and controlled to serve the interests of both the major state powers and the TNCs that dominate global trade and investment. Thus 'liberalisation' is best seen as a code word for the process of restructuring the world economy that works largely in the favour of and is determined by the state managers and corporate interests of the G7 states.

10.  The fact that this social and economic restructuring is unevenly distributed is reflected in a number of ways. Most importantly, perhaps, the tendency for foreign direct investment (FDI) to the South to be dominated by a few key Southern states and regions (Dicken, 1992: 26). Thus the idea of a global economy must be treated with a great deal of caution. Most trade and investment takes place within the regions of North America, Japan and the European Union, a point that leads many writers to regard these developments as, thus far, 'triadization' rather than globalisation (Bienefeld, 1996).

11.  Interestingly when the World Bank issued its 2000 report on world development it led to the resignation of one of the report's main authors on the grounds that the US Treasury Secretary Larry Summers was trying to 'water down' the worst findings (see Atkinson, 2000).

12.  Caroline Thomas examines 'the Washington Consensus' in the first book in this series *Global Governance, Development and Human Security* (2000: 39–46). In addition see Waltz (1999: 2)

13.  The idea that markets are the best mechanism for promoting the efficient use of resources is an *a priori* assumption underpinning the ideology of neoliberal economic theory.

14.  Sovereignty and autonomy have always been largely fictitious concepts for the developing world, subject as they have been to the exploitation

of the core capitalist states. While formal juridical equality between sovereign states is a hallmark of the Westphalian system of international relations, the reality for most sovereign states has been dramatically different. When viewed in systemic terms, the concepts of sovereignty and autonomy have to be significantly rethought as nation-states have always been subject to a complex array of factors that have shaped their histories, such things as the structure of global capitalism into a system marked by a core, a semi-periphery and a periphery, as well as the geopolitical structure of inter-state relations.

15. Chomsky (1997) notes an example of a firm hanging signs in front of plants where unions were trying to organise that read 'Mexico Transfer Jobs'.

16. The daily turnover of foreign exchange transactions is over US $1.5 trillion of which 15 per cent corresponds to actual commodity trade and the rest is speculative capital flows (Hahnel, 1999: 16; Henwood, 1997: Chapter 2).

17. The obvious problem with this claim concerns the question of judgement and enforcement. There are no independent institutions in international relations capable of judging fairly and consistently the behaviour of all states and enforcing laws as necessary. Such a power is the preserve of the core capitalist states, primarily NATO under US leadership. Thus the criminal actions of the core capitalist states are never going to be punished by an international court of justice without major transformations in the structure of world order (Evans, 1998; Chomsky, 1999).

18. Whilst I do not wish to go into this point in particular depth here, an interesting overlap exists between this neoliberal theme about pluralism and power and postmodern social thought with its emphasis upon the indeterminacy of interests and the circularity of social power in which we can no longer talk meaningfully about hierarchies of power, only unstable and changing formations. By way of contrast I would suggest that it is difficult to make sense of developments in the communications industry without recourse to notions of hierarchy and structure.

19. The issue of media effects is perhaps the most contested aspect of media analysis and for good reasons. Conventional Humean models of causation that have tended to dominate modern social science have looked for invariant law-like relations that hold in the social domain. As a consequence, orthodox models of media effects fail to take into account that social systems are open systems of activity where the kind of equilibrium conditions found in the laboratory of the natural sciences do not obtain. Thus, as realist social theory has argued with persuasive force, laws in the social realm are tendencies, and causality is a complex outcome involving relationships between phenomena that will be both necessary *and* contingent. As such, we should not expect to see uniform effects through media messages, but a more complex picture of the relationship between media institutions and the agents who interpret such messages and ideas. For a more detailed analysis of these points see Bhaskar (1979). The media remain our primary providers of information about the world. They may not tell us how to think, but they do tell us what to think about. This may be

a less powerful claim about the media but it is still important and as Jamieson's work shows, politicians certainly *believe* that the media have great significance over their own success or failure.

20. The idea of a market society is conceptually problematic under capitalism in that capitalist markets are, as Polanyi noted (1944), fundamentally anti-social, which is precisely why states moved to regulate them in the first place. Left to themselves, capitalist markets destroy societies. The power struggles of capitalist markets are inimical to substantive human values such as solidarity and sympathy and so it is difficult to see how they can be reconciled in practice.

## *Chapter 3*

1. As quoted in *Collins Concise Dictionary of Quotations*, 1987, London, Wm. Collins and Son, p. 15.
2. Before any postmodernists get too excited at this theoretical flaw I mean to use the term 'evolution' in its non-teleological sense, that is, meaning change and transformation. I accept that even this qualification may be too much for some tender hearts.
3. Knowledge may be said to be relative in that it changes over time. Our knowledge about environmental damage to the planet is a good example of this. However, our knowledge is not relative in the sense that at any given time we act on the belief that all claims to knowledge about the natural and social world are equally plausible. Thus we always must, and do, judge between contrasting knowledge claims about the world and we use empirical evidence as well as logic in order to do so.
4. In which Putnam observes, 'what we call "truth" depends both on what there is (the way things are) and on the contribution of the thinker (the mind).'
5. As Andrew Sayer has noted, if anything goes, then everything stays.
6. See Wilkin (2000) for an account of the Seattle protests and the use of NIT.
7. As the Report says, 'more than a quarter of the developing world's people still live in poverty as measured by the human poverty index introduced in this Report. About a third – 1.3 billion people – live on incomes of less than $1 a day' (p. 3). Similarly it goes on to add that over 100 million people in the industrial world live below the income poverty level, set at half the median income.
8. The WTO is a crucial institution because it is both symbolically and practically representative of the ways in which global capitalism and the inter-state system have become intertwined. Thus, it is seen as perfectly 'normal' that private corporate interests should quite literally be able to buy seats at the negotiating table with trade ministers and the like, presumably on the assumption that whatever is in the interest of these private companies is somehow akin to the public interest. Some interesting facts that give some sense of the balance of power at the WTO:

   • The US has over 250 negotiators at the WTO in Geneva. Thirty of the remaining 134 members of the WTO cannot afford to base anyone at

the WTO in Geneva, let alone afford the costs of expensive trade lawyers to help set out and defend their position on global trade.
- The US has filed 30 per cent of all disputes with the WTO, winning 90 per cent of them. Three-quarters of the membership have filed one-fifth of the complaints.
- Decision making at the WTO is dominated by the quad countries: the US, the European Union, Japan and Canada, all of whose trade representatives work closely with their respective corporate representatives.
- Corporate sponsorship of the Seattle summit gained access to various ministers and meetings for private companies, with a sliding scale in accord with the size of their donations:

| | |
|---|---|
| Emerald Level | $250,000 |
| Diamond Level | $150,000–249,000 |
| Platinum Level | $75,000–149,999 |
| Gold Level | $25,000–74,999 |
| Silver Level | $10,000–24,999 |
| Bronze Level | $5,000–9,999 |

For more details see the World Development Movement (1999); Mokhiber and Weissmann (1999) who note that corporations paid US$ 9–10 million of the costs of funding the Seattle summit.
9. Margaret Archer conceptualises this question of structure and agency in philosophical realist terms as being a concern with 'positions-practices' (1995).

## Chapter 4

1. Global economic growth has slowed by roughly half since the mid-1970s, roughly the period when the neoliberal agenda was beginning to take off. As measured by the gini coefficient, global inequality has increased steadily between countries since the mid-1970s, see Park and Brat (1995). See 'labor today', by Brecher et al. (1999) for an account of the changing patterns of global inequality and the slowing of global economic growth since the mid-1970s. For recent comment on the ways in which these pressures are being felt by sections of the US workforce see Conlin (1999). On global poverty and inequality see Shalom (1999); and *The Economist* (2000a).

## Chapter 5

1. On the subject of laws in social science as tendencies rather than invariant relations see Sayer (1992: Chapters 3 and 4).
2. In systemic terms this factor, the tendency to pursue profit, is one of the principles that helps to define capitalism. Simply, it is one property that helps to make capitalism distinct from, say, feudalism, or a slave economy.
3. The national interest is a contested concept that has different meanings to different approaches to international relations. For example, for realists, it tends to mean the collective interests and identities of a body

of people (the nation) and a particular territory and its institutions (the state). Such an assumption assumes that what this group of people share in common as a community is more important than factors that might divide them such as class, gender, ethnicity, and so on. Alternately, and more realistically I would argue, in practice that which constitutes the national interest of the core capitalist states tends to be determined primarily in relation to the most powerful political and economic sectors of those communities. As Wallerstein would note, this tends to be presented as common interests when they are in fact primarily the interests of the elite that dominate the core capitalist states, and as such the idea of a national interest is an ideological device that serves to misrepresent the real nature of existing social relations (Wallerstein, 1991).

4.  The attack upon trade unions by states and the weakening of the power of working people to resist the demands of private capitalist corporations is one of the defining features of the neoliberal agenda. For neoliberals, the ability of working people to defend themselves from the violence of capitalism is seen as a 'market distortion'.

5.  Even calling your party 'The Worker's Party' is to invite unwanted attention and trouble! The names of political parties are, of course, significant in terms of political culture, as we have seen recently in Britain with the rebranding of 'New Labour' under the Blair administration (see Ramsay, 1998).

6.  Lest I be accused of latent Eurocentrism here, I am happy to note that corruption would seem to be endemic to pretty much all political systems around the world. Everywhere, from the US, Germany, Italy and Britain through to Indonesia, China and Brazil, corruption is part and parcel of political life (Kaufmann, 1997). Before neoliberals get too twitchy here, blaming it on those pesky politicians, it is worth noting that corruption takes two, invariably commercial *and* political interests, as the recent scandals affecting Germany reveal (*Economist*, 1998a). What is more interesting in many respects is that the real scandal of politics in the era of neoliberal global governance is one in which the interests of private companies are seen as being practically synonymous with the public interest. This extends into the formal process of elections (for example, see Borger, 2000). The fact that companies can sponsor the WTO meeting at Seattle, buy access to ministers and so on, and that this is considered to be normal politics, is quite breathtaking. This is a process that we saw with NAFTA when the mainstream media and politicians saw nothing wrong with business 'lobbying' the US Congress to vote to approve the treaty, whereas the lobbying by trade unions to represent their members' interests which they saw as being threatened by NAFTA was an affront to the democratic process. For an account of this see Noam Chomsky (1993). This ethos says a great deal about the political culture generated by neoliberal global governance.

7.  Remember, as Gellner (1995) noted, relativism is the problem we face, not the answer to the problem.

8.  The question of media effects on audiences is very well documented. For introductory debates see Inglis (1990: Chapter 7); or Grossberg et al. (1998: Chapters 8–11).

9.   I am not entirely in agreement here with Herman and McChesney's assumptions as to the conservatism of corporate capitalists as a coherent class. It seems to be more complex than this in that capitalists are undoubtedly committed to liberal freedoms embodied in rights, not least because in having more wealth and property they gain from their preservation disproportionately.
10.  For a neoliberal critique of the BBC, see the recent interview with Rupert Murdoch, in which he says of the BBC that *'there are a lot of people there who enjoy the status quo, the self appointed elite who hate anything happening that changes Britain'* (Hagerty, 1999).

## Chapter 6

1.   Colin Hay (2000) notes that the so-called 'Washington Consensus' was a product of coercion on the part of powerful states' representatives and corporate agents.
2.   For an account of the 'Washington Consensus' see the World Bank (2000: 63).
3.   See my earlier comments about the relationship between necessary and contingent factors.

# Bibliography

Albert, M. and Hahnel, R. 1990. *The Political Economy of Participatory Economics*, New Jersey, Princeton University Press.

Albright, M. 2000. 'Democracy in the Balkans'
<http://secretary.state.gov/www/statements/2000/000629.html>

Alleyne, M.D. 1995. *International Power and International Communication*, London, Macmillan.

Altschull, J. H. 1995. *Agents of Power: The Media and Public Policy*, New York, Longman.

Amin, S. 1997. *Capitalism in the Age of Globalisation*, London: Zed Books.

Anderson, B. 1983 and 1992 editions. *Imagined Communities*, London, Verso.

Apple Jnr, R.W. 2000. 'The state of the Union', *New York Times*, 28 January.

Archer, M. 1995. *Realist Social Theory: The Morphogenetic Approach*, Cambridge, Cambridge University Press.

Arrighi, G., Hopkins, T. and Wallerstein, I. 1989. *Antisystemic Movements*, London, Verso.

Atkinson, M. 2000. 'Poverty row author quits World Bank', *Guardian*, 15 June
<http://www.guardianunlimited.co.uk/Archive/Article/0,4273,4029590,00.html>

Bagdikian, B. 1992. *The Media Monopoly*, Boston, Beacon Press.

Bain, W.W. 1999. 'Against crusading: The ethic of human security and Canadian foreign policy', *Canadian Foreign Policy*, Vol. 6, No. 3, Spring.

Baldwin, D.A. 1993. *Neorealism and Neoliberalism: The Contemporary Debate*, New York, Columbia University Press.

Bates, S. 1998. 'Belgium PM acquires 'absolutist' powers', *Guardian*, 5 August.

Baylis, J. and Smith, S. (eds) 1997. *The Globalisation of World Politics*, Oxford, Oxford University Press.

BBC News Online. 1998. 'Row over Blair's Murdoch intervention', 27 March
<http://news6.thdo.bbc.co.uk/hi/english/uk/politics/newsid_70000/70597.stm>

BBC News Online. 1999a. 'Business: the Economy Frankfurt Shares Surge', 12 March
<http://news.bbc.co.uk/hi/english/business/the_economy/newsid_295000/295989.stm>

BBC News Online. 1999b. 'Business: The Economy - Internet helps make rich richer', 21 June
<http://news.bbc.co.uk/hi/english/business/the_economy/newsid_374000/374134.stm>

Beirne, M. and Ramsay, H. (eds) 1992. *Information Technology and Workplace Democracy*, London, Routledge.

Bello, W. et al. 1993. *Dark Victory*, London, Pluto Press.

Bendix, R. 1969. *Nation-Building and Citizenship*, New York, Anchor Books.

Berg, A. and Berg, E. 1997. 'Methods of privatisation', *Journal of International Affairs*, Vol. 50, No. 2, Winter.

Beyer, P. 1994. *Religion and Globalisation*, London, Sage.

Bhaskar, R. 1979. *The Possibility of Naturalism*, Hemel Hempstead, Harvester Wheatsheaf.

Bienefeld, M. 1996. 'Is a strong national economy a utopian goal at the end of the twentieth century?', in, Boyer, R. and Drache, D. (eds), *States Against Markets*, London, Routledge.

Blum, W. 1986. *The CIA: A Forgotten History*, London, Zed Books.

Bogart, L. 1994. 'Consumer Games', *Index on Censorship*, September/October, No. 4/5.

Booth, K. 1991. 'Security and Emancipation', *Review of International Studies*, Vol. 17, No. 4.

Booth, K. and Smith, S. 1995. *International Relations Theory Today*, Cambridge, Polity Press.

Booth, K. Smith, S. and Zalewski, M (eds) 1996. *International Theory: Positivism and Beyond*, Cambridge, Cambridge University Press.

Borger, J. 2000. 'For sale: The race for the White House', *Guardian*, 7 January.

Bourdieu, P. 1998. *On Television and Journalism*, London, Pluto Press.

Boyd-Barrett, O. 1997. 'International communication and globalisation: Contradictions and direction', in Mohammadi, A. (ed.) 1997. *International Communication and Globalisation*, London, Sage.

Boyd-Barrett, O. and Tantanen, T. (eds) 1998. *The Globalisation of News*, London, Sage.

Boyer, R. and Drache, D. (eds) 1996. *States Against Markets*, London, Routledge.

Bradshaw, Y.W. and Wallace, M. 1996. *Global Inequalities*, California, Pine Forge.

Brady, R. 1937. *The Spirit and Structure of German Fascism*, London, Gollancz.

Brecher, J. et al. 1993. *Global Visions*, Boston, South End Press.

Brecher, J., Costello, T. and Smith, B. 1999. 'labor today', *ZNET* <http://www.zmag.org/ZMAG/articles/feb99brecher.htm>

Brittain, V. and Elliot, L. 1996. 'Close the gap between rich and poor', *Guardian*, 16 July.

Brown L. and Kane, H. 1995. *Full House: Reassessing the Earth's Population Carrying Capacity*, London, Earthscan.

Brown, S. 1995. *Postmodern Marketing II*, London, International Thomson Business Press.

Buckingham, L. 1999. 'A taxing enigma at the heart of News Corp', *Guardian*, 20 March.

Burchill, S. et al. (eds) 1996a. *Theories of International Relations*, London, Macmillan.

Burchill, S. 1996b. 'Liberal Internationalism', in S. Burchill et al. (eds), *Theories of International Relations*, London, Macmillan.

*Business Week*. 1998a. 'Clyde Prestowitz: Views from an old Japan trade hawk', 18 April <http://www.businessweek.com/1998/20/b3578009.htm>

*Business Week*. 1998b. 'Germany's Lafontaine talks, business trembles', 23 November <http://www.businesswek.com/1998/47/b3605179.htm>

Calhoun, C. (ed.) 1992. *Habermas and the Public Sphere*, Massachusetts, MIT Press.

Carey, A. 1997. *Taking the Risk out of Democracy: Corporate Propaganda Vs Freedom and Democracy*, Urbana, Illinois, University of Illinois Press.

Carr, E.H. 1995. *The Twenty Years Crisis*, London, Macmillan.

Carroll, R. 2000. 'Mayor Vs media baron', *Guardian*, 23 October.

Carrothers, T. 1999–2000. 'Civil society is crucial for economic success', *Foreign Policy*, Winter.

Castells, M. 1996. *The Rise of the Network Society*, Oxford, Blackwell.

Castells, M. 1998. *End of the Millennium*, New York, Blackwell.

Castles, S. and Miller, M.J. 1993. *The Age of Migration*, London, Macmillan.

Cavallo, D. 1999. 'The Global Observer', *Forbes*, 17 May
<http://www.forbes.com/global/1999/0517/0210014a.html>

Cavanagh, J., Wysham, D. and Arruda, M. (eds) 1994. *Beyond Bretton Woods*, London, Pluto Press.

Chomsky, N. 1973. *For Reason of State*, London, Penguin.

Chomsky, N. 1982. *Towards a New Cold War*, London, Sinclaire Browne.

Chomsky, N. 1987. 'Psychology and ideology', in *The Chomsky Reader*, London, Serpent's Tail Press.

Chomsky, N. 1993. *Year 501: The Conquest Continues*, London, Verso.

Chomsky, N. 1994. *World Orders, Old and New*, London, Pluto Press.

Chomsky, N. 1997. 'Market democracy in a neoliberal order'
<http://www.zmag.org/Zmag/articles/nov97chomsky.htm>

Chomsky, N. 1998. *Profit over People: Neoliberalism and Global Order*, New York, Seven Stories Press.

Chomsky, N. 1999. *The New Military Humanism*, London, Pluto Press.

Chossudovsky, M. 1997. 'The global financial crisis', *Third World Resurgence*, No. 86, October.

Chossudovsky, M. 1997. *The Globalisation of Poverty*, London, Zed Books.

Collier, A. 1994. *Critical Realism: An Introduction to Roy Bhaskar's Philosophy*, London, Verso.

Collins, R. and Murroni, C. 1996. *New Media, New Policies: Media and Communications Strategies for the Future*, Cambridge, Polity Press.

Comor, E.A. (ed.) 1994. *The Global Political Economy of Communication*, London, Macmillan.

Conlin, M. 1999. 'Economic growth: Hey, what about us?', *Business Week*, 23 December.

Connolly, W. 1991. 'Democracy and Territoriality', *Millennium: Journal of International Studies*, Vol. 20, No. 3, Winter.

Connolly, W. 1989. *Political Theory and Modernity*, Oxford, Blackwell.

Copley, S. and Sutherland, K. (eds) 1995. *Adam Smith's Wealth of Nations*, Manchester, Manchester University Press.

Corbridge, S., Thrift, N. and Martin, R. (eds) 1994. *Money, Power and Space*, Oxford, Blackwell.

Cox, R. 1987. *Production, Power and World Order: Social forces in the making of history*, New York, Columbia University Press.

Cox, R. 1989. 'Production, the state and change in world order', in Czempial, E. and Rosenau, J.N. (eds), *Global Changes and Theoretical Challenges*, Massachusetts, Lexington Books.

Cox. R. 1996. 'Gramsci, hegemony and international relations: An essay in method', in his *Approaches to World Order*, Cambridge, Cambridge University Press.

Cox, R. W. 1999. 'Civil society at the end of the Millennium: Prospects for an alternative world order', *Review of International Studies*, January, Vol. 25, No 1.

Curran, J. 1991 'Mass media and democracy: A reappraisal', in Curran, J. and Gurevitch, M. (eds), *Mass Media and Society*, London, Edward Arnold.

Curran, J. and Gurevitch, M. (eds) 1991. *Mass Media and Society*, London, Edward Arnold.

Curran, J., Gurevitch, M. and Woollacott, J. (eds) 1977. *Mass Communication and Society*, London, Edward Arnold.
Curran, J. and Seaton, J. 1997. *Power Without Responsibility*, London, Routledge.
Czempial, E. and Rosenau, J.N. (eds) 1989. *Global Changes and Theoretical Challenges*, Massachusetts, Lexington Books.
Dahl, R. 1985. *A Preface to Economic Democracy*, Berkeley, University of California Press.
Davies, A. 1994. *Telecommunications and Politics*, London, Pinter Publishers.
Dawson, M. and Bellamy Foster, J. 1998. 'Virtual Capitalism', in R.W. McChesney et al., *Capitalism in the Information Age*, New York, Monthly Review Press.
De Waal, A. and Omaar, R. 1994. 'Can military intervention be "humanitarian"?', *Middle East Report*, Vol. 24, No. 2–3.
Denny, C. 2000. 'Internet promises salvation - or an even bigger knowledge gap', *Guardian*, 1 February.
Dicken, P. 1992 and 1998. *Global Shift: Transforming the world economy*, London, Paul Chapman.
Dicken, P. and Lloyd, P. 1990. *Location in Space: Theoretical perspectives in economic geography*, New York, Harper and Row.
Doyal, L and Gough, I. 1991. *A Theory of Human Need*, London, Macmillan.
Drache, D. 1996. 'From Keynes to K-Mart', in Boyer, R. and Drache, D. (eds) *States Against Markets*, London, Routledge.
Dunne, T. 1997, 'Realism', in Baylis, J. and Smith, S. (eds) *The Globalisation of World Politics*, Oxford, Oxford University Press.
Durham Peters, J. 1993. 'Distrust of Representation: Habermas on the Public Sphere', *Media, Culture and Society*, Vol. 15.
*Economist*. 1998a. 'Who really runs Germany?', 19 November
<http://www.economist.com/displayStory.cfm?Story_ID=177962&CFID=62812&CFTO KEN=26208078>
*Economist*. 1998b. 'The resources lie within', 7 November.
*Economist*. 1999. 'The surveillance society', 29 April
<http://www.economist.com/displayStory.cfm?Story_ID=202160&CFID=62812&CFTO KEN=26208078>
Economist. 2000a. 'Old battle; new strategy', 7 January
<http://www.economist.com/displayStory.cfm?Story_ID=272116&CFID=62812&CFTO KEN=26208078>
*Economist*. 2000b. 'The case for globalisation', 25 September
<http://www.economist.com/displayStory.cfm?Story_ID=374064&CFID=62812&CFTO KEN=26208078>
*Economist*. 2000c. 'The end of taxes?', 23 September
<http://www.economist.com/displayStory.cfm?Story_ID=375612&CFID=62812&CFTO KEN=26208078>
*Economist*. 2000d. 'Untangling e-conomics', 23 September
<http://www.economist.com/surveys/showsurvey.cfm?issue=20000923>
*Economist*. 2000e. 'Cross-border investment', 10 February.
*Economist*. 2000f. 'The next revolution', 22 June
<http://www.economist.com/displayStory.cfm?Story_ID=80746&CFID=62812&CFTO KEN=26208078>
*Economist*. 2000g. 'The Electric Revolution', 3 August
<http://www.economist.com/displayStory.cfm?Story_ID=28183&CFID=62812&CFTO KEN=26208078>

*Economist*. 2000h. 'From dot.com to dot.bomb', 29 June
<http://www.economist.com/displayStory.cfm?Story_ID=2807&CFID=62812&CFTOK EN=26208078>

*Economist*. 2000i. 'The beginning of a great adventure', 21 September
<http://www.economist.com/displayStory.cfm?Story_ID=375663&CFID=62812&CFTO KEN=26208078>

Elliot, L. and Atkinson, D. 1998. *The Age of Insecurity*, London, Verso.

Evans, H. 1997. 'The charge of freedom', *Guardian*, 2 June.

Evans, T. (ed.) 1998. *Human Rights Fifty Years On: A Reappraisal*, London, St. Martin's Press.

Eyre, R. 1999. 'Eyre's vision for the future', *Guardian*, 28 August.

Fay, B. 1975. *Social Theory and Political Practice*, London, Allen and Unwin.

Fay, B. 1987. *Critical Social Science*, Cambridge, Polity Press.

Feigenbaum, H. and Henig, J. 1997. 'Privatisation and Political theory', *Journal of International Affairs*, Vol. 50. No. 2, Winter.

Ferguson, M. (ed.) 1989. *Public Communication: The New Imperatives*, London, Sage.

Fleetwood, S. (ed.) 1999. *Critical Realism in economics: Development and debate*, London, Routledge.

Fones-Wolf, E. 1994, *Selling Free Enterprise: The Business assault on labour and Liberalism – 1945–60*, Illinois, University of Illinois Press.

*Fortune Global 500*. 1999. 'Industry snapshot'
<http://www.fortune.com/fortune/global500/indsnap/0,5980,IN|157,00.html>

Foucault, M. 1980. *Power/Knowledge*, Brighton, Harvester Wheatsheaf.

Franck, T. and Weisband, E. 1971, *Word Politics: Verbal Strategy among the Superpowers*, New York: Oxford University Press.

Frederick, H.H. 1992. *Global Communication and International Relations*, Belmont, California, Wadsworth.

Friedland, L.A. 1996. 'Electronic Democracy and the New Citizenship', *Media, Culture and Society*, Vol. 18.

Friedman, D. 1978. *The Machinery of Freedom: Guide to radical capitalism*, Lexington, Arlington House Publishers.

Friedman, M. 1962. *Capitalism and Freedom*, Chicago, University of Chicago Press.

Fukuyama, F. 1992. *The End of History and the last man*, London, Penguin.

Gamble, A. 1996. 'Hayek and the Left', *The Political Quarterly*, Vol. 67, No. 1, January–March.

Garnham, N. 1990. *Capitalism and Communication*, London, Sage.

Gates, B. 1995. *The Road Ahead*, New York, Viking Press.

Gates, B. 1999. *Business at the Speed of Thought: Using a digital nervous system*, London, Penguin.

Gellner, E. 1985. 'Concepts and Communities' in his *Relativism and the Social Sciences*, Cambridge, Cambridge University Press.

George, S. 2000. 'Fixing or Nixing the WTO', *Le Monde Diplomatique*, January <http://www.corpwatch.org/trac/feature/wto/6-george.html>

George, S. 1994. *A Fate Worse Than Debt*, London, Penguin.

Giddens, A. 1994. *Beyond Left and Right: The Future of Radical Politics*, Cambridge, Polity Press.

Giddens, A. 1999. *The Third Way: The renewal of social democracy*, Cambridge, Polity Press.

Gilbert, N. and Gilbert, B. 1989. *The Enabling State*, Oxford, Oxford University Press.

Gill, S. 1990. *American Hegemony and the Trilateral Commission*, Cambridge, Cambridge University Press.

Gill, S. 1995. 'Globalisation, Market Civilisation and Disciplinary Neoliberalism', *Millennium: Journal of International Studies*, Vol. 24, No. 3.

Gill, S. and Law, D. 1990. *The Global Political Economy*, Brighton, Harvester Wheatsheaf.

Gilmour, I. 1992. *Dancing with Dogma*, London, Simon and Schuster.

Gilpin, R. 1987. *The Political Economy of International Relations*, New Jersey, Princeton University Press.

Golding, P. 1992. 'Communicating Capitalism', *Media, Culture and Society*, Vol. 14.

Golding, P. and Harris, P. (eds) 1997. *Beyond Cultural Imperialism: Globalisation, Communication and the New International Order*, London, Sage.

Golding, P. and Middleton, S. 1982. *Images of Welfare*, Oxford, M. Robertson.

Golding, P. and Murdock, G. 1977. 'Capitalism, Communications and Class Relations', in Curran, J. et al. (eds), *Mass Communication and Society*, London, Edward Arnold.

Golding, P. and Murdock, G. 1991. 'Culture, Communication and Political Economy', in Curran, J. and Gurevitch M. (eds), *Mass Media and Society*, London, Edward Arnold.

Gowan, P. 1998. *Global Gamble*, London, Verso.

Granfield, A. 10-1-2000. 'Debt, what debt?', *Forbes*, 10 January <http://www.forbes.com/tool/html/00/Jan/0110/mu14.htm>

Gray, C. 1999. 'Clausewitz Rules OK?', *Review of International Studies*, December, Vol. 25.

Gray, J. 1998. *False Dawn: The Delusions of Global Capitalism*, London, Granta Press.

Greenslade, R. 2000a. 'Do we want to go large?', *Guardian*, 22 May.

Greenslade, R. 2000b. 'I'm a fig leaf for page 3', *Guardian*, 2 October.

Griffin, M., Viswanath, K. and Schwartz, D. 1994. 'Gender Advertising in the US and India: Exporting Cultural Stereotypes', *Media, Culture and Society*, Vol. 16.

Griffiths, M. 1992. *Realism, Idealism and International Relations*, London: Routledge.

Grossberg, L., Wartella, E. and Whitney, D.C., 1998. *MediaMaking*, London, Sage.

*Guardian*. 1996. 'Wapping: Ten Years On', 8 January.

Habermas, J. 1974. 'The Public Sphere', *New German Critique*, Vol. 3.

Habermas, J. 1979. *Communication and the Evolution of Society*, London, Heinemann Educational Press.

Habermas, J. 1989. *The Structural Transformation of the Public Sphere*, Oxford, Polity Press.

Habermas, J. 1999. 'Bestiality and Humanity: A war on the border between law and morality', *Die Zeit*, Vol. 54, No. 18, 29 April.

Hacker, K.L. 1996. 'Missing Links in the Evolution of Electronic Democracy', *Media, Culture and Society*, Vol. 18.

Hagerty, B. 1999. 'Blair, god and the net', interview with Rupert Murdoch, *Guardian*, 29 November.

Hague, B. and Loader, B. (eds) 1999. *Digital Democracy*, London, Routledge.

Hahnel, R. 1999. *Panic Rules: Everything you need to know about the global economy*, Canada, Global Image.

Halliday, F. 1994. *Rethinking International Relations*, London, Macmillan.

Halliday, F. and Rosenberg, J. 1988. 'Interview with Ken Waltz', *Review of International Studies*, Vol. 24, No. 3.

Hamelink, C.J. 1994a. *The Politics of World Communication*, London, Sage.

Hamelink, C.J. 1994b. *Trends in World Communication*, Penang, Third World Network.

Hamelink, C.J. 1997. 'International communication: Global market and morality', in Mohammadi, A. (ed.), *International Communication and Globalisation*, London, Sage.

Harris, N. 1986. *The End of the Third World*, London, Penguin.

Harvey, D. 1973. *Social Justice and the City*, London, Edward Arnold.

Hay, C. 2000. 'Contemporary capitalism: globalisation, regionalisation and the persistence of national variation', *Review of International Studies*, Vol. 26, No. 4, October.

Hayek, F. A. 1944. *The Road to Serfdom*, London, Routledge.

Heinbecker, P. 1999. 'Human Security', *Canadian Institute of International Affairs*, Vol. 56, No. 2, January–March.

Held, D. 1987. *Models of Democracy*, Cambridge, Polity Press.

Held, D. 1995. *Democracy and the Global Order*, Cambridge, Polity Press.

Held, D., McGrew, A., Goldblatt, D., and Perraton, J. 1999. *Global Transformations*, Cambridge, Polity Press.

Henwood, D. 1993. 'Paying for Health', *Left Business Observer*, No. 57, February <http://www.panix.com/~dhenwood/Paying-for-health.html>

Henwood, D. 1997. *Wall Street*, London, Verso.

Henwood, D. 1998a. 'Asia Melts', *Left Business Observer*, No. 81, January <http://www.panix.com/~dhenwood/AsiaMelts.html>

Henwood, D. 1998b. 'Crisis Update', *Left Business Observer* No. 85, September <http://www.panix.com/~dhenwood/CrisisUpdate.html>

Henwood, D. 1999. 'Antiglobalisation', *Left Business Observer*, Issue 71, January <http://www.panix.com/~dhenwood/Globalization.html>

Herman, E. and Chomsky, N. 1988, *Manufacturing Consent: The Political Economy of the Mass Media*, New York, Pantheon Books.

Herman, E. and McChesney, R.W. 1997. *The Global Media*, London, Cassell.

Hewson, M. 1994. '*Surveillance and the Global Political Economy*', in Comor, E.A. (ed.), *The Global Political Economy of Communication*, London, Macmillan.

Hewson, M. and Sinclaire, T. (eds) 1999. *Approaches to Global Governance Theory*, New York, State University of New York Press.

Hirst, P. and Thompson, G. 1996. *Globalisation in Question*, Cambridge, Polity Press.

Holton, R. 1992. *Economy and Society*, London Routledge.

Huber, P. 1999. 'Wealth and Poverty', *Forbes*, 27 December.

Hutchison, D. 1999. *Media Policy: An introduction*, Oxford, Blackwell.

Ignatieff, M. 1995. 'On Civil Society', *Foreign Affairs*, March/April.

Inglis, F. 1990. *Media Theory*, Oxford, Blackwell.

ILO (International Labour Organisation) 1997. 'Amsterdam conference targets child slavery – Press release', 25 February <http://www.ilo.org/public/english/bureau/inf/pr/97-3.htm>

Jackall, R. (ed.) 1995. *Propaganda*, London, Macmillan.

Jackall, R. and Hirota, J. 1995. 'America's first propaganda ministry', in Jackall, R. (ed.), *Propaganda*, London, Macmillan.

Jackson, B. 1994, *Poverty and the Planet*, London, Penguin Books.

Jameson, F. 1991. 'The cultural logic of late capitalism', in his, *Postmodernism, or, The Cultural Logic of Late Capitalism*, London, Verso.

Jamieson, K.H. 1992. *Dirty Politics: Deception, Distraction and Democracy*, New York, Oxford University Press.

Jamieson, K.H. 1997. *The Interplay of Influence*, Belmont, California, Wadsworth Press.

Jenkins, R. 1987. *Transnational Corporations and Uneven Development*, London, Methuen.

Jensen, J. 1990. *Redeeming Modernity: Contradictions in Media Criticism*, London, Sage.

Jessop, B. 1974. *Traditionalism, Conservatism and British Political Culture*, London, Allen and Unwin.

*Journal of International Affairs* 1997. 'Special Issue: Privatisation', Vol. 50, No. 2, Winter.

Kanth, R. 1999. 'Against Eurocentred epistemologies', in Fleetwood, S. (ed.), *Critical Realism in Economics: Development and debate*, London, Routledge.

Kaufmann, D. 1997. 'Corruption: The facts', *Foreign Policy*, Summer.

Keane, J. 1991. *Media and Democracy*, Cambridge, Polity Press.

Keck, M.E. 1992a. *The Workers' Party and Democratisation in Brazil*, Yale, Yale University Press.

Keck, M.E. 1992b. 'Brazil's Socialism as Radical Democracy', *NACLA*, May.

Keegan, V. 1996. 'Highway robbery by the super-rich', *Guardian*, 22 July.

Kegley, C.W. 1995. *Controversies in IR theory: Realism and the Neoliberal Challenge*, New York, St. Martin's Press.

Kelley, D. and Donway, R. 1990. 'Liberalism and Free Speech', in Lichtenberg, J. (ed.), *Democracy and the Mass Media*, Cambridge, Cambridge University Press.

Kennan, G. 1966. 'Our duty to ourselves', in G. Stourzh et al. (eds), *Readings in American Democracy*, New York, Oxford University Press.

Keohane, R.O. 1986, *Neorealism and its Critics*, New York, Columbia University Press.

Kettle, M. 2000. 'Getting the measure of America's poor', *Guardian*, 6 November.

Knightley, P. 1999. 'How much of what NATO and the MOD tells us can we believe?', *Guardian*, 15 April.

Knightley, P. 2000. *The First Casualty: The war correspondent as hero and myth-maker from the Crimea to Kosovo*, London, Prion Books.

Kobrin, S.J. 1998. 'The MAI and the clash of globalisations', *Foreign Policy*, Fall.

Koss, S. 1990. *The Rise and Fall of the Political Press in Britain*, London, Fontana.

Krugman, P. 1989. 'The case for stabilising exchange rates', *Oxford Review of Economic Policy*, Vol. 15, No. 3.

Krugman, P. 1999. 'The Speculators Ball', in his *The Accidental Theorist*, London, Penguin Books.

Lazonick, W. 1991. *Business Organisation and the Myth of the Market Economy*, Cambridge, Cambridge University Press.

Lichtenberg, J. (ed.) 1990. *Democracy and the Mass Media*, Cambridge, Cambridge University Press.

Linklater, A. 1998. *The Transformation of Political Community*, South Carolina, University of South Carolina Press.

Lippmann, W. 1955. *The Public Philosophy*, Boston, Mentor Books.

Little, R. 1995. 'International relations and the triumph of capitalism', in Booth, K. and Smith, S. (eds), *International Relations Theory Today*, Cambridge, Polity Press.

Locksley, G. 1986. 'Information Technology And Capitalist Development', *Capital and Class*, Vol. 27.

Lovering, J. 1987. 'Militarism, Capitalism and the Nation-State: Towards a realist synthesis', *Environment and Planning D: Society and Space*, Vol. 5.

Lubasz, H. 1995. 'Adam Smith and the "free market"', in Copley, S. and Sutherland, K. (eds), *Adam Smith's Wealth of Nations*, Manchester, Manchester University Press.

Lukes, S. 1974. *Power: A Radical View*, London, Macmillan.

Luthens, S. 1999. 'Labour and the WTO', *Corporate Watch*
<http://www.igc.org/trac/feature/wto/4-laborwto.html>

MacDonald, J.F. 1985. *Television and the Red Menace*, New York, Praeger.

Macintyre, A. 1987. *After Virtue: A Study in Moral Theory*, London, Gerald Duckworth and Co.

Manicas, P.T. 1987. *A History and Philosophy of the Social Sciences*, Oxford, Blackwell.

Mann, M. 1986. *The Sources of Social Power: Volume 1*, Cambridge, Cambridge University Press.

Mann, M. 1996. 'Authoritarian and Liberal Militarism', in K. Booth et al. (eds), *International Theory: Positivism and Beyond*, Cambridge, Cambridge University Press.

Mazzocco, D.W. 1994. *Networks of Power: Corporate TV's Threat to Democracy*, Boston, South End Press.

McChesney, R.W. 1993. *Telecommunications, Mass Media and Democracy: The battle for control of U.S. broadcasting 1928–35*, New York, Oxford University Press.

McChesney, R.W. 1999. 'The new global media', *The Nation*, 29 November,
<http://past.thenation.com/cgibin/framizer.cgi?url=http://past.thenation.com/1999/9
91129.shtml>

McChesney, R.W., Woods, E.M. and Bellamy Foster, J. 1998. *Capitalism in the Information Age*, New York, Monthly Review Press.

McLaughlin, L. 1993. 'Feminism, The Public Sphere, Media and Democracy', *Media, Culture and Society*, Vol. 15.

McLean, I. 1989. *Democracy and New Technology*, Cambridge, Polity Press.

McManus, J. 1994. *Market-Driven Journalism*, London, Sage.

McNair, B. 1995, *An Introduction to Political Communication*, London, Routledge.

McNair, B. 1997, *News and Journalism in the UK*, London, Routledge.

Meiskins, P. 1998. 'Work, New Technology and Capitalism', in McChesney, R.W. et al. (eds), *Capitalism and the Information Age*, New York, Monthly Review Press.

Melody, W.H. 1994. 'The information society', in Comor, E.A. (ed.) *The Global Political Economy of Communication*, London, Macmillan.

Melrose, D. 1985. *Nicaragua: The threat of a good example*, Oxford, Oxfam Books.

151  Th151 Th154154   The154  The Political Economy of Global Communication

Merrien, F.-X. 1998. 'Governance and modern welfare states', *International Social Science Journal*, No. 155, March.
Mills, C.W. 1995. 'The Mass Society', in Jackall, R. (ed.) *Propaganda*, London, Macmillan.
Mohammadi, A. (ed.) 1997. *International Communication and Globalisation*, London, Sage.
Moisy, C. 1997. 'Myths of the global information village', *Foreign Policy*, Summer.
Mokhiber, R. and Weissmann, R. 1999. 'Corporate capitalism at the WTO', *Corporate Watch*, 26 October
<http://www.igc.org/trac/feature/wto/2-hospitality.html>
Moore, B. 1973. *Social Origins of Dictatorship and Democracy*, London, Penguin.
Moore, N. 1997. 'Neoliberal or *Dirigiste*? Policies for an information society', *The Political Quarterly*, Vol. 68, No. 3, July–September.
Mosco, V. 1996. *The Political Economy of Communication*, London, Sage.
Mosco, V. and Wasko, J. (eds) 1988. *The Political Economy of Information*, Wisconsin, University of Wisconsin Press.
Mowlana, H. 1996. *Global Communication in Transition: The end of diversity?*, London, Sage.
Mulgan, G. 1991. *Communication and Control*, Cambridge, Polity Press.
Murdoch, R. 1994. *The Century of Networking*, St. Leonard's, New South Wales, Centre for Independent Studies.
Murdoch, R. 1995. 'The Empire Strikes Back', *Guardian*, 22 April.
Murdock, G. 1993. 'Communication and the constitution of modernity', in *Media, Culture and Society*, Vol. 15.
Murphy, C. 1994. *International Organisation and Industrial Change: Global Governance since 1850*, Cambridge, Polity Press.
*NACLA* 1994. 'Mexico out of balance', Vol. XXVIII, No. 1, July/August.
*NACLA* 1995. 'Brazil: the persistence of inequality', May/June, Special Issue.
*NACLA* 1996. 'Privilege and Power in Fujimori's Peru', Vol. XXX, No. 1, July/August.
Negrine, R. 1996. *Politics and the Mass Media in Britain*, London, Routledge.
Nicholson, M. 1998. 'Realism and Utopianism Revisited', in T. Dunne et al. (eds), *The 80 Year Crisis Revisited*, Cambridge, Cambridge University Press.
Norris, C., Moran, J. and Armstrong, G. (eds) 1998. *Surveillance, Closed Circuit TV and Social Control*, Aldershot, Ashgate.
Nozick, R. 1974. *Anarchy, State and Utopia*, Oxford, Blackwell.
Nye, J. and Owens, W. 1992. 'America's Information Edge', *Foreign Affairs*, Vol. 75, No. 2.
O'Neill, H. 1997. 'Globalisation, competitiveness and human security: Challenges for development policy and institutional change, *European Journal of Development Research*, Vol. 9, No. 1, June.
O'Neill, J. 1995. 'Polity, Economy, Neutrality', *Political Studies*, Vol. XLIII.
Ohmae, K. 1990. *The Borderless World*, New York, Harper Business Press.
Pagden, A. 1998. 'The genesis of "governance" and Enlightenment conceptions of the cosmopolitan world order', *International Social Science Journal*, Vol. 155, March.
Park, W. and Brat, D. 1995. 'A Global Kuznet's curve', *Kylos*, No. 48.
Petrella, R. 1996. ' Globalisation and Internationalisation: The dynamics of the emerging world order', in Boyer, R. and Drache, D. (eds), *States Against Markets*, London, Routledge.

Philo, G. (ed.) 1995. *Glasgow Media Group Reader Vol. II: Industry, Economy, War and Politics*, London, Routledge.

Pilger, J. 1992. *Distant Voices*, London, Vintage.

Plant, R. 1988. *Citizenship, Rights and Socialism*, London, Fabian Society.

Plant, R. 1991. *Modern Political Thought*, Oxford, Blackwell.

Polanyi, K. 1944. *The Great Transformation*, Boston, Beacon Press.

Popper, K. 1962. *The Open Society and its enemies: Vol. II*, London, Routledge.

Poster, M. 1995. *The Second Media Age*, Cambridge, Polity Press.

Potter, D. (ed.) 1997. *Democratisation*, Cambridge, Polity Press.

Preston, W., Herman, E. and Schiller, H.I. 1989. *Hope and Folly: The United States and UNESCO 1945–1985*, Minneapolis, University of Minnesota Press.

Putnam, H. 1993. *Reason, Truth and History*, Cambridge, Cambridge University Press.

Putnam, H. 1995. *Pragmatism*, Oxford, Blackwell.

Raghavan, C. 1990. *Recolonisation: GATT, The Uruguay Round and the Third World*, Penang, Third World Network.

Ramsay, R. 1998. *Prawn Cocktail Party: the hidden power behind New Labour*, London, Vision Paperbacks.

Rawls, J. 1973. *A Theory of Justice*, London, Oxford University Press.

Reich, R. 1992. *The Work of Nations: Preparing ourselves for C21 Capitalism*, New York, Vintage Books.

Ricupero, R. 1997. 'Privatisation, the state and international institutions', *Journal of International Affairs*, Vol. 50, No. 2, Winter.

Robertson, R. 1992, *Globalisation: Social Theory and Global Culture*, London, Sage.

Rodrigues, I.J. 1995. 'The CUT: New Unionism at the crossroad', *NACLA*, May/June.

Rodrik, D. 1997. 'Sense and nonsense in the globalisation debate', *Foreign Policy*, Summer.

Rorty, R. 1989. *Contingency, Irony and Solidarity*, Cambridge, Cambridge University Press.

Rorty, R. 1991. 'Solidarity or Objectivity?', in his *Objectivity, Relativism and Truth*, Cambridge, Cambridge University Press.

Rosenau, J. 1971. *The Scientific Study of Foreign Policy*, New York, The Free Press.

Rothkopf, D. 1997. 'In praise of cultural imperialism?', *Foreign Policy*, June.

Sader, E. and Silverstein, K. 1991. *Without fear of being happy: Lula, The Worker's Party and Brazil*, London: Verso.

Said, E. 1978. *Orientalism*, London, Penguin.

Sassen, S. 1991. *The Global City: New York, London, Tokyo*, New Jersey, Princeton University Press.

Saunders, F.S. 2000. *The Cultural Cold War: The CIA and the world of arts and letters*, New York, New Press.

Sayer, A. 1995. *Radical Political Economy*, Oxford, Blackwell.

Sayer, A. 2000. *Realism and Social Science*, London, Sage.

Sayer, A. and Walker, R. 1992. *The New Social Economy: Reworking the Division of Labour*, New York, Blackwell.

Sayer, A. 1992. *Method in Social Science*, London, Routledge.

Sayer, D. 1989. *The Violence of Abstraction*, Oxford, Blackwell.

Schiller, H. 1989, *Culture Inc.*, New York, Oxford University Press.

Schlesinger, P. 1991. *Media, State and Nation: Political Violence and Collective Identities*, London, Sage.

Schlesinger, P. and Kevin, D. 2000. 'Can the European Union become a sphere of publics?', in Eriksen, E.O. and Fossum, J.E. (eds), *Democracy in the European Union*, London, Routledge.

Scholte, J. 2000. *Globalisation: A critical introduction*, London, Macmillan.

Sclove, R.E. 1995. *Democracy and Technology*, New York, Guildford Press.

Seabright, P. 2000. 'What's wrong with the WTO', *London Review of Books*. Vol. 22, No. 2, 20 January.

Seenan, G. 1999. 'CCTV "fails to cut crime and anxiety"', *Guardian*, 15 July <http://www.guardianunlimited.co.uk/Archive/Article/0,4273,3883342,00.html>

Seymour-Ure, C. 1996, *The British Press and Broadcasting since 1945*, Oxford, Blackwell.

Shalom, S. 1999. 'The state of the world', 14 September <http://www.zmag.org/Zsustainers/Zdaily/1999-09/14shalom.htm>

Shaw, M. 1994. *Global Society and International Relations*, Cambridge, Polity Press.

Shiva, V. 1987. 'The violence of reductionist science', *Alternatives*, Vol. 12, No. 2, April.

Shiva, V. 1989. *Staying Alive: Women, Ecology and Development*, London, Zed Books.

Shiva, V. 1999. 'Who owns the WTO?', *Corporate Watch* <http://www.igc.org/trac/feature/wto/6-shiva.html>

Sivanandan, A. 1990. *Communities of Resistance*, London, Verso.

Sklar, H. 1999. 'Brother, can you spare a billion?', *Z Magazine*, December <http://www.lol.shareworld.com/Zmag/articles/dec1999sklar.htm>

Skocpol, T. 1979. *States and Social Revolution*, Cambridge, Cambridge University Press.

Slevin, J. 2000. *The Internet and Society*, Cambridge, Polity Press.

Smith, A. 1991. *National Identity*, London, Penguin Books.

Smith, S. 1995. 'The self-images of a discipline', in Booth, K. and Smith, S. (eds), *International Relations Theory Today*, Cambridge, Polity Press.

Smith, S. 1996. 'Positivism and Beyond', in K. Booth et al. (eds), *International Theory: Positivism and Beyond*, Cambridge, Cambridge University Press.

Solomon, N. 2000. 'AOL Time Warner: Calling the faithful to their knees', *ZNET*, 21 January <http://www.zmag.org/Zsustainers/Zdaily/2000-01/21solomon.htm>

Soros, G. 1999. *Crisis of Global Capitalism*, New York, Warner.

Spero, J. E. 1990. *The Politics of International Economic Relations*, New York, St. Martin's Press.

Squires, J. (ed.) 1993. *Principled Positions*, London, Lawrence and Wishart.

Statewatch. 2000. 'homepage' <http://www.statewatch.org/index1.html>

Stourzh, G. et al. (eds) 1966. *Readings in American Democracy*, New York, Oxford University Press.

Streeton, P. 1999. 'Ten years of human development', *UN Human Development Report 1999*, New York, Oxford University Press.

Talbott, S. 1996, 'Democracy and the National Interest', *Foreign Affairs*, November–December.

Tavares, R. 1995. 'Land and Democracy: Reconsidering the agrarian question', *NACLA*, May/June.

Taylor, C. 1985. 'Interpretation and the sciences of man', in his *Philosophy and the Human Sciences: Philosophical Papers 2*, Cambridge, Cambridge University Press.

Taylor, P. 1997. *Global Communications: International Affairs and the Media since 1945*, London, Routledge.

Teather, D. 2000. 'Now Kingston needs a good deal', *Guardian*, 26 January <http://www.guardian.co.uk/Archive/Article/0,4273,3955062,00.html>

*Third World Resurgence*, 1993. 'From GATT to WTO or GATT 2', Issue 29/30, January–February.

*Third World Resurgence*, 1994. 'A world in social crisis', Issue 52, December.

*Third World Resurgence*, 1995. 'The struggle against biopiracy', Issue 63, November.

*Third World Resurgence*, 1997. 'Patent battle hots up: Community rights Vs Corporations', Issue 84, August.

Thomas, C. 1999. 'Where is the Third World now?', *Review of International Studies*, Vol. 25, December.

Thomas, C. 2000. *Global Governance, Development and Human Security*, London, Pluto Press.

Thomas, C. and Wilkin, P. 1997. *Globalisation and the South*, London, Macmillan.

Thomas, R. 1996. 'Wage gap a threat to society', *Guardian*, 17 July.

Thompson, J.B. 1990. *Ideology and Modern Culture*, Cambridge, Polity Press.

Tilly, C. 1997. *Coercion, Capital and European States, AD 990-1990*, Oxford, Blackwell.

Tomlinson, J. 1991. *Cultural Imperialism: An introduction*, London, Pinter.

Tomlinson, J. 1997. 'Cultural globalisation and cultural imperialism', in Mohammadi, A. (ed.), *International Communication and Globalisation*, London, Sage.

Tunstall, J. and Palmer, M. 1991. *Media Moguls*, London, Routledge.

Turner, T. 1994. 'The mission thing', *Index on Censorship*, Issue 42, September/October.

UNCTAD 1999. *World Investment Report 1999: Foreign Direct Investment and the challenge of Development*, Switzerland, United Nations Publications.

UNDP 1994. *Human Development Report*, Oxford, Oxford University Press.

UNDP 1996. *Human Development Report*, Oxford, Oxford University Press.

UNDP 1997. *Human Development Report*, Oxford, Oxford University Press.

UNDP 1998. *Human Development Report*, Oxford, Oxford University Press.

UNDP 1999. *Human Development Report*, Oxford, Oxford University Press.

UNDP 2000. *Human Development Report*, Oxford, Oxford University Press.

UNESCO. 2000. *World Education Report 2000*, Paris, United Nations Publications.

Unger, S. 1991. 'The role of a free press in strengthening democracy', in Lichtenberg, J. (ed.), *Democracy and the Mass Media*, Cambridge, Cambridge University Press.

UNICEF 2000. *The State of the World's Children Report* <http://www.unicef.org/sowc00>

Van der Pijl, K. 1998. *Transnational Classes and International Relations*. London: Routledge.

Vandenberg, A. (ed.) 1999. *Citizenship and Democracy in a Global Era*, London, Macmillan.

158   The Political Economy of Global Communication

Vaz, K. 2000. 'The Caspian region: UK and international priorities'
<http://www.fco.gov.uk/news/speechtext.asp?3396>

Walker, M. 1999. 'Security first say the bureaucrats', *Guardian*, July 19
<http://www.guardian.co.uk/Archive/Article/0,4273,3884474,00.html>

Walker, R. 1995. 'California rages against the dying of the light', *New Left Review*, January–February.

Wallace, M. and Bradshaw, Y. 1996. *Global Inequalities*, Thousand Oaks, California, Pine Forge.

Wallerstein, I. 1974. *The Modern World System: Volume One*, Florida, The Academic Press.

Wallerstein, I. 1979. *The Capitalist World-Economy*, Cambridge, Cambridge University Press.

Wallerstein, I. 1991. *Geopolitics and Geoculture: Essays on the changing world system*, Cambridge, Cambridge University Press.

Wallerstein, I. 1995. *After Liberalism*, New York, New Press.

Wallerstein, I. 1999. *The End of the World as we know it*, Minnesota, University of Minnesota Press.

Waltz, K. 1959. *Man, The State and War*, New York, Columbia University Press.

Waltz, K. 1979. *Theory of International Politics*, Massachusetts, Addison-Wesley.

Waltz, K. 1986. 'Reflections on a Theory of International Politics: A response to my critics', in Keohane, R. O. (ed.), *Neorealism and its Critics*, New York, Columbia University Press.

Waltz, K. 1995, 'Realist thought and neo-realist theory', in Kegley, C. (ed.), *Controversies in IR Theory: Realism and the Neoliberal Challenge*, New York, St. Martin's Press.

Waltz, K. 1999. 'Globalisation and governance', *Political Science and Politics*, December <http://www.apsanet.org/PS/dec99/waltz.cfm>

Walzer, M. 1995. *Toward a Global Civil Society*, Providence, R.I. Berghahn Books.

Watkins, K. 1999. 'Let's have a bonfire of tariffs and hypocrisy', *Guardian*, 10 November
<http://www.guardianunlimited.co.uk/Archive/Article/0,4273,3928782,00.htm>

Wilhelm, D. 1990. *Global Communication and Political Power*, New Brunswick, Transaction Books.

Wilkin, P. 1996. 'New Myths for the South: Globalisation and the conflict between private power and freedom', *Third World Quarterly*, Vol. 17.

Wilkin, P. 1999. 'Chomsky and Foucault on Human Nature and Politics – An Essential Difference?', *Social Theory and Political Practice*, Vol. 25, No. 2, Summer.

Wilkin, P. 2000. 'Solidarity in a global age – Seattle and beyond', *Journal of World Systems Research*, Vol. VI, No. 1, Spring.

Williams, R. 1984. *The Long Revolution*, London, Penguin.

Wolin, S. 1961. 'The age of organisation and the sublimation of politics' in his *Politics and Vision*, London, Allen and Unwin.

Wood, E.M. 1995. *Democracy Against Capitalism*, Cambridge, Cambridge University Press.

World Bank 1990. *World Development Report 1990: Poverty*, Washington DC, World Bank.

World Bank 1999. *World Development Indicators 1999*, Washington DC, World Bank <http://www.unicef.org/sowc00/fig1.htm>

World Bank 2000. *World Development Report 2000*, Washington DC, World Bank <http://www.worldbank.org/poverty/wdrpoverty/report/index.htm>

World Development Movement 1999. 'Multinationals and the WTO', September <http://www.corpwatch.org/feature/wto/1-mncs.html>

World Trade Organization home page <http://www.wto.org>

World Trade Organization, 1997. *Background paper on Telecommunications*, Washington, DC, 6 March.

Wright, R. 1999. 'We're all one-worlders now', *Slate*, 12 December <http://slate.msn.co/earthling/97-04-24/earthling.asp>

Young, H. 1989. *One of Us: A Biography of Margaret Thatcher*, London, Macmillan.

Zapatistas, 1994. *Zapatista*, New York, Semiotext (e).

# Index